THE ULTIMATE DENTAL WEBSITE

The Formula to Get More Traffic,

Engagement and New Patients

January 2016

DOUG WILLIAMS

Table of Contents

Contents

Forward

By Doug Williams

Your website needs to look professional and inviting when a prospective patient comes by. They need to understand that you are the right dentist to help them. They need to understand what you do. Then they need to trust you. All of this in 2-3 seconds. How do you do that?

You will learn the best way to organize your web page, how to build trust, where to place call to actions so they get noticed and multiple ways to drive traffic to your website. You will also learn how to properly use your website and avoid HIPAA pitfalls.

I wrote this book specifically for my dentist clients so they would understand our process as we planned and built their websites. This is powerful information for any dental practice that wants to use their website to grow their practice.

Ten years ago it was easy to launch a website and optimize a website to attract traffic. Today the landscape is far more competitive and Google has made it much harder to manipulate the search results.

This is a book about how to plan your dental website using the methods and systems that I routinely use with my clients. We will go through the steps on how to properly plan and market your business on the web in a step by step process.

Grab a cup of coffee while you learn what it takes to create your own high impact website that will truly transform your dental practice.

The Digital Landscape

Over the past 25 years the business of dentistry has changed dramatically. Much of the change has been fueled by technology.

In the early 90's, dentists marketed themselves using yellow page ads in the phone directory or using newspaper ads. The World Wide Web was in its infancy.

In December of 1992 the entire Internet was made up of just 50 websites[1]. By 2015 this number has grown to over 900 million websites[2].

Today 87% of the US adults uses the Internet[3] and dental marketing has shifted from traditional to digital marketing. Printed phone books and classified ads are all but dead as everything has moved over to digital.

Dental practices now market themselves with Websites, Facebook fan pages, Twitter accounts and blogs. When someone wants an answer, they "Google it."

The practice website is at the core of your branding and marketing effort showing how your practice delivers the best clinical results and uses the latest available technologies.

Technology continues to drive change in your dental practice with precise and almost instant solutions.

Dental Technology Innovations

CAD / CAM machines take digital impressions, create virtual models and then fabricate porcelain or composite restorations in a single visit.

Bonding and use of composites provide tooth colored restorations.

New technology in dental implants allows for advanced mapping and evaluation of bone structure which improves placement and healing in patients.

Laser technology is used in many areas of dentistry from soft tissue lasers, curing, whitening, decay removal and more.

Digital technology with digital impression systems, 3D printing, intraoral cameras, and new uses for lasers and digital diagnostic systems are now expected by your dental patients.

How you market your dental practice continues to evolve and change at a dizzying pace.

Life is Moving Faster

Digital technology has permeated the life of your patients with the smartphones and tablets providing easy Internet access 24 /7. This means that websites can no longer be a separate mobile website like we saw just 3 years ago, but now websites need to be responsive. Responsive technology allows a website to reformat and display properly on any size device.

———————

Your digital marketing needs to reflect the quality of care and the technology that you use in your dental practice.

1.   WHY a New Website?

You have made the decision that you need a new website. Start by looking at <u>why</u> you made that decision. This is the "why" that we are talking about.

Usually this starts with an emotional reaction to your present website. You could be ashamed of the image it portrays of your practice. You could be disgusted at the lack of new patients your site produced. You may be stressed by missing your financial goals.

Whatever your "why" is, use it to shape the objectives and the results you want from your new website. Never lose sight of your motivation for creating the new website. If your website fails to address the "why," you will never be happy with it.

Once you have made the decision to replace or even create your first website, you need to start building a list of some rational, logical results that you want this new website to produce for your dental practice.

Websites Should Deliver Results

Why should your dental practice invest in a new website? The website should help you reach your business goals. A website should be planned to get specific results that will transform and grow your practice by attracting the best high value patients to come and take specific actions.

4 Key Factors

1.   **Website purpose**- This is your business objective such as acquire new patients, increase conversions of leads from other marketing, etc. Your website needs to have a single primary purpose.

2.   **Patient profile**- A clear understanding of your best patients. What are their motivations? What triggers their decision to book their first appointment? What makes them a high value patient?

3.   **Conversion**- Your site needs to present a credible image for business, your message needs to be clear and answer the problem visitors came to solve and you need get them to take action.

4.   **Traffic**- Your best results come from people already searching for the service you provide. You need a steady flow of qualified prospects that you can serve.

Building good website plan is much like building a business plan. Your website should be treated like a stand-alone business unit. The more effort you put into a formal plan with strategies and tactics, the more likely you will be to succeed.

Figure 1.1 the Website Planning Pyramid

The process of creating a great website is simple and straight forward. It is really about creating alignment with what you want your website to accomplish and the needs of your best patient. Your site needs to provide the solution path for your patients.

By this I mean that people search the web for a solution to a problem or a need. Your website needs to clearly show why you have the best solution and then you need to give them a way to take the next step toward their solution.

To really have an impact on your practice, your website must attract your best patients. You need to have a clear traffic strategy. You should develop multiple channels that will send patients your way.

Traffic can come from organic Search Engine Optimization (SEO), paid search engine ads such as Google AdWords, social media, patient referrals and traditional marketing methods such as radio, TV and direct mail.

Plan to Grow Your Practice

Before you start planning your website, start with basic strategic planning. Dental technology is changing quickly, and chances are that your market is pretty competitive.

Look at ways to reinvent your dental practice or add new technologies that will expand or improve your available treatments. Your competition will be doing this. If you don't, your competition will pass you by.

Chances are that you will want to structure your website marketing around your technologies and use these to help differentiate your practice.

Look at what is new in available dental technologies that fit your current practice. Then look at what your patients need and want. Look at the following breakthrough questions to generate ideas and opportunities for growth.

16 Breakthrough Questions

1. What new dental technologies are available that fit with your current dental specialty or dental special services.
2. What services are requested that you do not offer?
3. What has recently changed in the lives of your patients?
4. What are the 3 biggest worries or concerns that they have?
5. How have your patients' needs changed in the past two years? How will things change in the next two years?
6. What one thing would your patients change about you, your practice or your policies; what would it be?
7. What is most important to your patients: time, money or quality?
8. Why would patients choose to go to another dentist over your practice?
9. What are your patients favorite and least favorite services?
10. What could you do to make your patient dental visit a more enjoyable experience?
11. How could you improve the design, style, sounds, smells or other sensory experience for your dental patients?
12. What infuriates your patients today?
13. What one thing most frustrates your staff?
14. What additional products or services would your patients buy from you if they could?
15. What 3 things would your patients remove from your offering if they could?
16. What would you need to offer to get dental patients for life?

Website Purpose

Before you build your website, you need to ask yourself "Why I am building this website? What is the business reason for this site to exist? What is your website meant to do?" Here are 7 common purposes for a website.

1. Share information
2. Generate leads
3. Sell products online
4. Promote your brand
5. Interact with your patients
6. Build your email list
7. Recruit new staff

Before you start planning how you will approach your prospective patient, you need to understand what you want your website to do for you. What is your primary motive for creating your website?

The objective is not to generate traffic. It should not be a brochure that describes your practice. For your website to have an impact on your practice, you need to expect certain results from it. If you don't set goals, you can't achieve them.

You need to take inventory of your business assets and strengths that you want to build on. Look at your Unique Selling Proposition (USP). What advantages do you have over your competition? What benefits will people have in doing business with you? Remember that people make buying decisions based on the differences, not how you are the same as your competition.

Once you have a clear laser like focus on what your website should do, then you can build your strategies to get these results. You want to focus your entire website around achieving the business results you want from your website.

Develop a Patient Profile

The most important thing you can do to increase your conversion rate is to have a deep understanding of your most targeted patient. You want a deep understanding of who they are and what is their motivation for seeking treatment?

As you build up your patient profiles, ask yourself these questions.

1.   Who are your best patients? What do you know about them? I.e. demographic, type of treatment, long term patients, referral source.

2.   Why would they come? What are their motivations?

3.   What makes them make an appointment? What is the trigger that will cause them to get treatment?

Your website can be designed to address your best patient persona on your home page. You can construct multiple selling sequences for your other patient personas. You will likely develop your messaging on your website to encourage your best patient and perhaps discourage those you do not want to target.

Get Visitors to Take Action

Your website needs to be designed to be a conversion engine. The more focused your website is toward a single purpose, the better your results. The more possible actions a visitor to your website can take, the lower your conversion rate.

What affects conversion rates?

- Your design should instill confidence and trust.
- Use simple intuitive menus and navigation.
- Create Headlines and sub-headlines to tell your story.
- Your web page content should educate
- Your content should flow like a well-orchestrated story.
- Address your patient's concerns. Show them a path to a solution
- Communicate your message and support your page headlines with compelling pictures or graphics.
- Use videos to educate and visualize results.

- Provide a clear and visible action for visitors to take such as request an appointment now.
- Your website should look trustworthy.

Traffic

Your website should be designed to attract prospects from Google search. Do this by doing keyword research and then building these keywords into your website's content.

Develop multiple traffic strategies such as social media and PPC advertising.

———————

Effective websites are designed for maximum impact on your business. In other words, they get results.

2. What Do They Want?

When a visitor comes to your website, what do they want? Why did they come? Are they a highly coveted high value patient looking for a special service?

This really is a study in psychology. You need to understand what your patients are seeking, what they are thinking, what their motivations are and what their triggers to take action are. In this chapter we will discuss the concept of your best patient, developing a profile for your patient and ways to get insight into what your visitors are searching for.

Some will come looking for information; some will arrive ready to book appointments. People seeking information may become patients once they get enough information. These shoppers will want to know why what you offer is different, why it is better.

Your website may have several different types of shoppers. Each will likely have different buying criteria. Here are 4 types of shoppers.

1. **Price shopper**- They make their decision based on price and is bargain hunters. They treat services as commodities and put little emphasis on the quality of the solution.

2.   **Technology shopper-** They want state of the art technologies with the latest treatments. They will have a clearly defined need that a dental technology will solve.

3.   **Solutions shopper-** They are searching for a solution to a critical issue such as an acute toothache, loose teeth, or bleeding gums.

4.   **Custom shopper-** They want a customized solution that is tailored to their situation. They avoid stock solutions and they rely on the dental practitioner's skill to craft a unique solution for them.

Best Patients

You will want to segment your patient base and decide what the ideal patient for your practice is. Are they looking for high value services that will be lucrative for you?

Are there certain types of patients that will likely become long term repeat patients that will have a higher lifetime value?

Some patients have urgent needs for emergency treatment and they may be very easy to get to book appointments, but may not be your ideal patient that you are looking for.

Who are your best patients? What do you know about them? How old are they? How well educated? What do you know about their income level? Do they live or work in a particular area? Are they from a particular industry? What job position do they hold?

Are they searching for a particular treatment or perhaps some sort of financing solution?

What personal desires are they trying to satisfy? What are the things that bother them or their pain points? Are you closely matching their needs with what you have to offer?

What makes them willing to proceed with advanced treatments? What is the trigger that will cause them to buy? By showing that you clearly understand their pain, people become much more open to take action. You want to present a website that clearly solves their issue or concern.

The Patient Persona

You will likely construct profiles or personas for your patients. A Patient Persona is a fictitious, specific and concrete representation of your targeted website visitors. This is a way to put a personal, human face on a group of visitors that are seeking certain goals.

Your website can be designed to address your best patient persona on your home page. You can construct multiple selling sequences for your other patient personas. You will likely develop your messaging on your website to encourage your best patient and perhaps discourage those you do not want to target.

As an example a dental clinic website may have two distinct groups of people they market to. There are general dentistry patients that need to long-term dental maintenance and then there may be dental implant patients seeking the latest implant technology with CBCT scanning technology. Each will have very different needs and each requires a different selling sequence with a different call to action.

Your website needs to connect with your patient. A great connection comes from good communication. Good communication isn't talking; it comes from a deep understanding. It comes from using a shared language, a shared vocabulary, imagery, symbols and behavior. Content on your site needs to be both useful and aligned with the needs of your visitors.

What kinds of things should you include in a patient persona? See the example on following page.

1. Background- name and nickname, photo, age, gender, education level and work experience.
2. Describe the individual- personality, timid or bold, communication style, computer skills.
3. Problem identification- what your visitor is seeking, what is the purpose, what are their

expectations, goals and what is the problem to be solved?

4.   Motivation level- urgency, desires, price vs. quality.

Example: Meet Sally Jones

 Sally Jones is a 37 year old working mother of two teenagers. Sally and her family have just moved into a new home in the North Atlanta upscale community of Buckhead. She is married to an executive and has a household income of $180,000. Sally drives a luxury car and has a career as a real estate broker. She has a college degree and keeps current on news and events even with her busy schedule.

She is active on Facebook and uses her smartphone for emails and texting as well as for doing web research. Sally is an active networker and always recommends people she works with to her clients.

Sally is very computer literate and is very comfortable doing research online. In her job she has learned to make instant decisions based on her first impression.

Sally makes the decisions in her family for selecting the health care providers. One of her urgent priorities is to select a dental clinic for herself and her family. She is looking for general dentistry for her kids and is interested in finding a cosmetic dentist to help improve her smile.

Her priorities for selecting a dentist is in getting the highest quality care that will fit into her busy schedule. She wants access to the latest technologies.

She wants a dental office that is professional and modern in appearance. She is looking for a practice where she can book appointments online. Saturday appointment availability is one important criteria in selecting a dentist.

Psychology of Search

When people search on a search engine, what do they search for? Generally speaking, people search with a definite purpose. They have a question to be answered, information to research or something to buy.

Search engines are a tool for people to access information.

What are people searching for? It is whatever is impacting their life at that moment. They could be searching for a dentist after moving; they could be searching for a solution for a painful toothache.

Figure 2.1 Keywords

Using Keyword Research

As a marketer, we look at usage patterns of how people search for specific products or services. We look at past searches to predict how people will search in the future.

Let's look at how people may look for a plumber. We start by looking at all plumbing related searches. We categorized all these phrases to look for patterns.

1. Fixtures- 54.3% of searches were for fixtures (kitchen sinks, faucets, bathroom fixtures)
2. Plumber- 19.1% of searches were for a plumber (plumber, plumbing contractor)

3. Parts- 16.3% were for parts (plumbing supplies, plumbing parts)
4. Problem- 10.3% of searches were for an urgent problem (broken pipe, toilet repair)

Phrases related to fixtures and parts would be more suited to a plumbing products store that sells to do-it-yourselfers. People most often search for a plumber using the word plumber, usually along with a city name. They also search frequently based on the nature of the problem.

This would mean a plumber's website should not only be optimized for "plumber + city" but also for the types of problems he solves or installations he does.

The same psychology applies to how people may search for a dentist. We looked at searches for dentist[4] and they fell into 5 categories.

1. Treatment information – 47.7% (dental implants, teeth whitening).
2. Search for a dentist – 30.5% (dentist, orthodontist)
3. Researching a condition – 7.6% (toothache, gum disease)
4. Price related – 7.5% (dental implant cost, free dental care)
5. Product related – 6.7% (dental floss, teeth whitening gel)

This highlights the importance of having a well-developed patient education section for your website. Each treatment and each condition should have its own page. Since people search for dentists locally, you will want your address on every page.

To be really effective though, it all needs to be original content so the search engines will be willing to display your content in their search engine results. Avoid using "stock content" that is easy to deploy, but almost worthless in attracting search engine traffic. The search engines see this stock content as "duplicate content" that exists on hundreds of other dentist sites.

Search engines actively filter out this duplicate content from their search results.

Keywords used in optimizing your website are linked to buyer psychology and conversion strategies. Search phrases give a view into what a searcher is thinking.

Search Psychology

Local Intent: Including a city or other geographic reference indicates buyers that are searching for local businesses. Dental practices (even national chains) are searched for locally.

Phrase Length: People begin their buying process in the research phase with short 1-2 word keyword phrases. They are searching for more general phrases. As they get closer to making a buying decision, the search phrases become longer and more specific. Buyer keywords are typically 3-5 words or even longer.

Customer Words: You will want to think like your patients, not an industry expert. Did you know most realtors instinctively want to be found for "real estate for sale" yet most people actually search for "homes for sale"?

Focused Content: Focus your website on solving a narrow set of problems. This will be more attractive to someone seeking a solution provider. Specialists are more trusted than generalists.

We find that keyword research done at a very early phase of the project gives great insight into the problems people are trying to solve and helps develop patient profiles. These same keywords help develop messaging across the website and to develop a content plan. Keyword research also helps in developing the SEO plan.

Keyword Selection Criteria

1. Relevance- Select keywords first based on relevance. Are they looking for what you provide?

2. Buyer Phrases- Look for phrases that indicate visitors are ready to take action.

THE ULTIMATE DENTAL WEBSITE

31 | Page

3. Search Volume- Once you have narrowed your list of relevant buyer phrases, then choose based on the highest search volumes.

Keyword Research Tools

There are free and paid keyword research tools. Some do a better job or are faster to use. All work by querying search engines such as Google for their information. Google offers its own free keyword tool.

1. Google keyword planner (Free). You will need to Login with Google and create an AdWords account.
   https://adwords.google.com/KeywordPlanner

2. Wordtracker (Paid) Free trial available.
   http://www.wordtracker.com/

3. Market Samurai (Paid)
   http://www.noblesamurai.com/products.php

———————

Marketing to your best patients is a study in psychology. You need to understand what your patients are seeking, what they are thinking, what their motivations are and what their triggers to take action are.

3 Image and Branding

How you brand your dental practice is very important in building a memorable business in the minds of your patients. Your website needs to reflect your branding strategies for your practice.

Importance of Branding

Is branding important in something as routine and unglamorous as a general dentistry practice? Absolutely!

In 2003 Nick Friedman[5] and a couple of college buddies bought an old cargo van. Nick was a senior at Pomona College. They started the unglamorous business of moving, deliveries and junk removal to earn extra money for college. Like most freight companies this business was unmemorable and blended in with hundreds of other companies. They earned just $8000 in their first summer of operation.

Nick's challenge was how to differentiate his hauling business. By the spring of 2004, Nick came up with the idea to rebrand themselves as "College Hunks Hauling Junk." This idea grew from a single truck to a fleet of 50 trucks and 33 franchises nationwide in just 10 years.

Nick's service was not new, how he branded and positioned his business from something unsexy to something sexy was his innovation.

Website Branding

How important is the "look" of your website? Your website is a reflection of your branding. It is how people see and judge your dental practice. Is it a modern reflection of your technology?

According to the findings from the Stanford Web Credibility Project, 75% of web users admit making judgments about the credibility of an organization based on the design of its website.[6]

Would you buy a new Rolex for $25 from a stranger? ...probably not. The price may be enticing, but you wouldn't trust that it was real. People do judge your business by its cover.

Your digital branding is more than just how your website looks. It is the sum of all the online perceptions, memories and experiences that people have of your products or company. Your digital branding strategy is more than making your brand memorable; it is about creating a connection and an expectation that you provide the best solution.

Difference between Branding and Marketing

Branding is about creating the unique name, image, story, expectations and values. Traditional marketing strategies are telling people why they should buy. Branding is the emotional arm of marketing. Branding is more strategic while sales and marketing is more tactical. Successful branding is emotional and creates customer loyalty.

Emotional

Logical

BRANDING   VS.   **MARKETING**

Qualitative, Art, Logo, Colors, Design, Identity, Intangible, Motivates, Promises, Symbol, Communicates, Awareness, Trademarks, Shapes, Trust

Science, Quantitative, Target, Segmentation, Market Study, Advertising, Promotion, Pricing, Channels, Positioning, Advertising, Research, SEO

Figure 3.1 Branding vs. Marketing

6 Digital Branding Strategy Elements

1. Targeting- The message is carefully developed to reach the right audience. Your solution should create a high interest and appeal to this segment. You should have a clear understanding of their needs and wants. Conduct market analysis and surveys to gather data.

2. Logo- The logo is the single most important visual representation of your company's brand identity. A good logo is memorable, unique and simple; it conveys a message to your target audience. Use of taglines in logos is diminishing because they tend to be too limiting.

3. Domain- Memorable and easy to remember domain names are very important to the website brand identity. Google.com and target.com are examples of simple prominent brands where the domain matches their brand.

 Try and use .COM to appear as a market leader since 76% of all domains in the US are .COM[7].

4. Personality- This includes voice, message, style and design. There needs to be a consistent brand personality used in all communication. It is the brand personality that engages and interacts with your targeted audience. The voice and messaging used in copywriting can range from formal and highly technical to friendly and inviting.

5. Visibility- Create strategies to boost your brand's visibility to your target audience. Visibility strategies can include SEO, social media marketing, PR, online and offline advertising and promotional giveaways. Use of multiple channels increases effectiveness.

6. Consistency- Be consistent in your use of logo, colors and even how you present your company name. All

websites, emails, letterhead, etc. should use consistent branding.

A successful digital branding strategy creates an emotional connection with your prospective and current customers. It helps attract and retain loyal customers. Branding establishes a premium value that people are willing to pay more for.

What makes a good logo?

Your logo is a visual icon of your branding. You use your logo on your website, business cards, letterhead, brochures and in your email. A great logo is memorable, creates a visual impact and helps your company become easily remembered.

So, what makes a great logo? It is simple, distinctive, represents the company and has the illusion of action.

1. Simple means that it is not overly complex, can be reduced to a small size on a business card and doesn't have many complex and competing elements. Simple also means good contrast and a bold look.
2. Distinctive means being unique and memorable, graphic (not just letters), not being cluttered in look and something that has a unique look. The colors, shape and font should be used in combination to help the business stand out and not blend in.

3. Relevant- Your logo design should symbolize your business and create a positive first impression. Concentrate on an abstract image to represent the feel of your company's business. Shapes, curves and symmetry can convey meaning.

4. Illusion of action means the logo has the appearance of motion and doesn't just sit there. This draws in your visitor's attention. By adding in the image of a partially turned key, shapes or textures a logo can be made to show action. Think of the Nike Swoosh to illustrate running shoes.

5. Color and Contrast- A great logo must be easily seen and attract attention. Your choice of colors communicates emotion and is an important part of your message. Contrast can be created using colors, texture and use of white space.

A simple great logo may not be easy or quick to create, but it is powerful in your company's branding for marketing strategies or Internet marketing.

 Need a new logo at a reasonable price? Use 99designs.com. For $300 you will get multiple designers competing and submitting logo designs.

Selecting a Domain Name

Selecting a domain name is as much about branding as is creating a logo for your business. Your domain should be memorable, recognizable and easy to type out.

1. Name Recognition- In most cases the domain name should match the company name. This may mean the full company name (wellsfargo.com, or bestbuy.com) or using a recognizable abbreviation such as IBM.com or HP.com. You can also choose a keyword driven domain like GiftBaskets.com which is owned by Hayneedle Inc.

2. Choose a .COM- People naturally think first of a .COM before a .NET, .INFO or .BIZ. That is because in the US, 76% of all domains registered are .COM. If you use something other than a .COM, it forces you to emphasize the end (.NET or .BIZ) of your domain instead of the name itself when marketing. This hurts your branding strategy.

3. Keep it Short- This makes it easier to type. Don't sacrifice making it memorable though. Later I will tell you how. I made this mistake when I formed my company.

4. Easy to Type- Avoid the use of hyphens because people will forget to type them in. If your domain purpose is strictly for SEO, hyphens are fine. Including numbers makes your domain harder to type. Easy to remember should outweigh easy to type.

5. Check Copyright- Avoid copyright infringement by checking copyright.gov. Your domain name should be relevant to your business name or business

model (products, services) to be defensible against infringement.

6. Check History- Use the Wayback Machine www.archive.org to see what other site may have been on that domain. Sometimes these past sites may cause a problem for your future website.

It is very important to choose the right domain name. Let me use my own company as an example.

In 2002 I started up my business as a consulting company and selected Doug Williams and Associates as my business name. Once my company name was established, I went searching for a suitable domain. The obvious one "DougWilliams.com" was taken. I knew shorter domain names were better, so I abbreviated my company name to "DWAssoc.com." Seems logical doesn't It?

This was a big mistake. Even though I did some things right – it was short, represented the company and was a .COM – I overlooked a few important details. It wasn't memorable and people couldn't remember what it stood for; every time someone asked me for my email address, I found myself repeating the spelling three or four times. The domain wouldn't stick in their memory and didn't strengthen my brand.

I finally went out and purchased "DougWilliams.com" and paid a premium price for it. This was the best decision I could have made. Even though it was longer, it was memorable and reinforced my brand. Now, I never have to repeat the spelling of my email address to anyone.

Get your own domain and send email using that domain and avoid using Gmail, Hotmail, AOL or Comcast emails. These are fine for personal email, but for business you want to appear more stable, reliable, and professional. It's best to use yourname @yourcompany.com.

Choice of Color in Branding

Color is another powerful communicator that you can use in branding and should not be taken for granted. It can trigger emotional responses based on nationality, past experiences, and even personal preference. There have been numerous studies done on how different colors affect the majority of online visitors. In general, red, orange, and yellow are exciting colors while purple, blue and green are calming ones.

Below are example colors and what they tend to convey:

Black: Elegance, formality, mystery, death and style.

Blue: Stability, truth, professionalism, dignity, trust, peace and coolness.

Brown: Endurance, casual, earthy, poverty and tradition.

Gold: Expensive, prestige, wisdom, attainment, high quality.

Gray: Conservatism, seriousness and enhances messages of other colors.

Green: Safety, harmony, freshness, nature, health and wealth.

Orange: Enthusiasm, cheerfulness, creativity, playfulness, vibrant and heat.

Purple: Power, wealth, nobility, intelligence, magic, sensuality and spirituality.

Red: Boldness, excitement, urgency, desire, intensity, danger and love.

Silver: Scientific, cold, prestige, sleekness, modernity and high-tech.

White: Cleanliness, purity, simplicity, peace and innocence.

Yellow: Attention-grabbing, happiness, warmth, energy, joy and optimism.

Take some time to think through what image and personality you want to reflect to the world.

———————

The six major elements of digital branding include: targeting, logo, domain name, personality, visibility and consistency.

4   Closing the Deal

Most websites today do little to generate leads or sales. The reason is because they are not designed to engage or interact with their visitors. Most are just a brochure with basic information about the business. The hope is somebody will be interested enough to pick up the phone and call.

What separates the average website from top producing websites? It is focusing and targeting the needs of your patient.

For a dentist website, it is very important to first establish trust and credibility. Most people will equate the quality of the website with the quality of the dental care they will receive. A modern up to date website equals receiving modern up to date dental care.

Once you address their questions or concerns, your website should be designed to encourage action.

Your website's appearance, messaging and your offer need to target their questions, concerns and needs. You need to understand the psychology and motivation of these visitors.

People come to your website to solve a specific problem.

Ask These 4 Questions

1. **What**- What is the focus of your site? What services or perhaps products do you offer? Your website, like your business needs to have a clear purpose. What problems do you solve for your patients? This could be patient education or a quiz to test their knowledge.

    How is it unique and better than your competition? What benefits will your patient experience by coming to you? Your home page should address and answer those questions.

2. **Who**- Who are your best patients? Are they the health care decision maker? If not, who is and what are their motivations? What do you know about them? How old are they? How well educated? Income level? Live or work in a specific area? From a particular industry? Do they have special health concerns? How tech savvy are they? Create a realistic profile of your best patient. Use this persona to visualize what their triggers are.

3. **Why**- Why would they come? What are their motivations? What personal desires are they trying to satisfy? What are their pain points? Are you closely matching their needs with what you have to offer? Are they coming for a smile makeover? To solve a recurring dental bridge repair?

4. **Action**- What makes them schedule that appointment?
    What is the trigger that will cause them to act? By
    showing that you clearly understand their pain, people
    become much more open to action. You want to
    present a website that clearly solves their issue. Make it
    clear and easy this path to action.

Drive your visitors toward a desired action. Online viewers
can only focus on one thing at a time. If you present many
options, then they won't react to any of them.

Getting people who come to your site to take specific
actions is called conversion optimization.

"Conversion" means to persuade individuals you have
attracted to your website to voluntarily undertake one or
more action steps. Depending upon the goals you have
established for your website, this may mean you want them
to sign up for a newsletter, make an appointment request,
fill out a form or perhaps simply contact you.

Incorporating just the right blend of logic, emotion, science,
psychology and art into a website is the formula to attract
prospects who are interested in what you offer, have a
current need, can afford to buy now, and will buy again in
the future.

Business-to-Consumer Buyers: Dental patients are
considered B2C buyers. These type of buyers tend to make
a more impulsive decision based on their current need. This

includes product, value, cost, and status. Buying is based on a desire with a very short decision making time. Most consumers will buy regularly from stores and locations that they like. B2C marketing needs to build trust and loyalty with their customers.

The Selling Sequence

Every business including your dental practice has a sales process that best guides your prospects into becoming patients. Your website is no different. You need to design your selling sequence that will grab their attention, build their interest and then get them to take action.

How you present information to visitors to convert them from a prospect to a customer is your sales process. Your selling sequence should follow AIDA. This is Attention, Interest, Desire and then Action. This has been in use as a sales training tool for over a hundred years. For good reason, it works.

The typical selling sequence starts by making the prospect aware of your service. You then spend time generating interest in what you are selling. You then stimulate the desire to possess the results of your service. Finally you encourage the prospect to buy.

A visitor begins by arriving to your website because they are searching for a solution to their need. If you start by demonstrating what your service can do, then they may not want that capability you are offering. If you first create interest and then desire for your treatment, then they feel they have to have what you are selling.

You have to develop the need. You do this by first asking questions in a way where your service is the natural answer to the question. Do this with the right questions and then you develop a genuine need for your service.

If you have several pricing levels, which do you present first? You would present your highest priced, premium priced products of course.

The airlines are pros at this. Think of how you enter the plane on the way to Economy. First you get on the plane and walk through First Class. You see the wide comfortable seats, all the amenities, even drinks being served before takeoff. Next you march past business class; then you arrive in Economy.

Pricing for First Class gives sticker shock, and most of us say no to the high prices. Then every time we enter the plane, we are guided through the sequence of Attention, then Interest and then Desire. This helps trigger Action when we finally get fed up with Economy and "bang", they have a sell.

You may need to create multiple patient personas. You can then design separate optimal selling sequences and then guide each persona through their buying process.

To develop your selling sequence you need to thoroughly understand your patient, what problem they are trying to solve and what their buying criteria are. You will need to adapt this general 10 step sales process to your website.

1. Identify your patient(s). You may need to develop multiple personas if you have several different types of patients that you market to.
2. How are you going to get interested prospects to your website?
3. What specific problem is each potential patient trying to find a solution for?
4. How does your product or service solve this problem? How is it unique and better than your competition? What benefits will your patient experience by buying from you?
5. What action do you want the visitor to take that would constitute success for you? How will you measure this?
6. How will you grab their attention and pique a potential patient's interest?
7. What concerns will a patient have that might cause them to put off a purchase? What can you do to build trust and reduce risk for a prospect?
8. What is the best way to present what you sell to the prospect? This should be as a solution to their problem and in a way that benefits them the most.

9. What is the trigger that will cause a prospect to buy? How do you overcome objections? How will you close the sale?
10. How will you service and follow up with these customers so you can turn them into repeat buyers?

As you plan your website, develop a selling sequence for each type of patient. Think about these steps as potentially separate web pages that you want to guide your visitor through.

Call to Actions

Your call-to-action needs to answer three questions.

1. **What?** What should they do? What action do you want them to take? Buy? Request a quote? Make an appointment? Sign-up?
2. **Why?** Why should they do it? Why should they trust you? How will it benefit them?
3. **How?** How do they take action? What is the next step?

5 attributes of a great call to action

1. Compelling- Make sure it satisfies a real need your visitor has. Use action oriented phrases such a "Book Now" or "Join Today."
2. Visible- Location is very important. Make it clearly visible and above the fold. Use colors that make it stand

out. On your home page, the upper right quadrant is prime territory for your call to action. It is more easily seen there.

3. Clarity- Keep it simple. Use short bulleted phrases. Don't clutter it up with too much text. Use simple graphics. Use ample white space.

4. Urgency- Create a sense of urgency to encourage immediate action. Limit the time or the quantity. Have an expiration date or label it as a limited time offer. You could make the offer available for the first 30 buyers.

5. Incentive- Offer a premium or reward for taking immediate action. This could be "Act now and receive..." Use an incentive that will appeal to your best buyer. This will help attract your targeted customer.

As you plan your website you will want to create a list of all possible actions that you want visitors to do. This could be to sign up for a free report, book an appointment or even call for more information. You will want to prioritize this list from the most important to the least important.

You will make your highest priority action the most visible and the most compelling.

Do People Trust your Website?

The single most important factor is first impression. Does your website look professional, organized and credible? People do judge a book by its cover. If your website looks like it was put together by an amateur, then that will be their perception of your business.

A study by researchers in Canada[8] showed that people form lasting judgments about the usability and credibility of a website in as little as 1/20th of a second. The reaction is a physiological and emotional response based on color, images, page load speed and organization. This first impression was not based on informational content.

A well-organized website is inviting and encourages people to come in and look around. Avoid strong and oppressive colors. Design with a minimum number of different fonts.

It is no difference with the brick and mortar stores that you shop in. Would you prefer to shop at a small store with a few items for sale, where the merchandise is not well organized, the shopping area not well lit, things are hard to find and where the checkout stand is a long complicated process?

Or would you rather shop at a store with good selection, well organized into departments, well-lit with wide aisles and a quick and easy checkout?

Make your website inviting to your visitor.

Use videos whenever possible. Visitors like to view video content. Add educational videos to allow people to visualize the result of a dental procedure. Videos are more compelling and communicate better than just images.

Your website needs to develop that instant trust that comes from that visual first impression. Then follow up with more signs they should trust you. Here are more ideas.

Appearance: The design of the website must be professional, uncluttered and have a neat visual appearance. Content and navigation must be organized and clear. Use high quality images to communicate your message.

Transactional Assurances: Show visitors there is no risk in doing interacting with your office. Provide assurances with privacy policies, guarantees, forms of payments accepted, return policies and trust logos. Provide point of action assurances with brief statements or links to your policies on privacy, guarantees and returns. Include your phone number and address on every page.

Authority Symbols: Your website must contain symbols of authority and credibility. People will immediately trust someone with a badge and a gun or a doctor in a white smock. With visual assurances people will make quick decisions with very limited information. For dental sites use photos of doctors in white coats. Add trust logos such as BBBonline or industry associations.

Social Proof: Provide third party recommendations with video and written testimonials. Integrate social reviews and comments using product reviews, ratings, consumer feedback, wish-lists, favorites, blogs, forums or chat rooms.

For maximum social proof, use a service that gathers positive reviews on your practice from around the web and allows you to display them in one place with an easy to post widget.

Closing the deal on your website uses what is called Conversion Rate Optimization. This is a blend of art and science. Your website must be professional and credible; it must be trustworthy, solve their problem and have a clear path to action.

———————

Every business including your dental practice has a sales process that best guides your prospects into becoming patients. Your website is no different.

5 Size-up Your Competition

Probably the most important step in planning your new website is to spend some time looking at other dental websites.

If you are an orthodontist, then you need to look at other orthodontist websites both in your area and in other major cities around the nation.

Every website will have aspects that you really like and that you hate. Keep careful notes of the website addresses and specifically the things you really like (or hate).

It is in looking at your competition's websites that your vision will become clear on how you will want your website to look and what calls to action you will want. This is one of the most important steps in planning your new website.

You want your website to be better than your competitors. You can get ideas for designs, layouts, call-to-actions, offers, functionality and how they are attracting traffic.

Remember your patients will be searching through a great many websites and comparing your website to your competition. The objective is to pick and choose the best ideas and improve on them so that your dental practice will be the obvious choice to go to.

How to select competitive websites

Start by creating a list of companies that you consider your direct competition. Limit this to only 3-5 competing dentists. Locate their websites and add these to your list.

You want to choose others by doing searches on Google.

Go to the keyword research that you did from chapter 2. You will want to pick the 5 best phrases that describe the services or products that you provide. These will become the "power phrases" that you will want to use in uncovering your competition.

This will be the same way your patients will be searching for you. You want to be seeing what they see.

To find competitors do a Google search using your "power keywords". Limit yourself to websites you find on the first two pages of Google.

As you do this search and you may notice the websites coming up are not a competitor to what you offer, if this is the case, then you may want to substitute a different keyword phrase that brings up better results. Make a note of this substitution so you can use this as you create your SEO page plan in chapter 6.

In the first pass you will be quickly going through these websites and sorting the good ones that you like from the "ugly" ones that you don't like.

Be prepared for a lot of "ugly" websites. Usually I reject at least 90% of the websites I look at in this first sort. If you are real picky, then you may reject 98% of the websites.

The goal in this first pass is to create a pool of good websites. You will look at these and select the best websites to become your reference websites. These will help guide the web designer in building your new website.

What to Look for in These Competitor Websites

The first pass as I said is to sort the good from the ugly. You are not trying to find the perfect website, only good ones. As you look closely at the good ones later, you will find pieces or elements that you really like that you want to include into your website.

This first sort is a quick visual sort and I look for three things to label a website as "good".

1. First Impression

2. Good layout

3. Clear call-to-actions

First impression- What is your initial reaction in the first 1-2 seconds? Does the page load quickly? This will be an emotional "I like it" or "I hate it". If you hate it, go onto the next website, if you like it try and figure out why.

The design should look professional but not overpowering. Do they see the most important things first?

Good Layout- This includes the page structure or where the elements are placed. Is it well organized? Is the navigation understandable? How clearly is the message presented? Can you find the information you need without scrolling down the page?

Clear call-to-action- Are there clear actions for visitors to take? This could be to request an appointment, signup for a newsletter or to call. Are the calls to actions placed so you can see them on the home page without scrolling down? Best practices are to place the call to actions in the upper right quadrant of the home page. See the example on the next page.

If you like a particular website for all three of these categories, then you will want to save it for further analysis.

An easy way to save these is to take a screenshot and paste them onto a Word document or into PowerPoint.

Looking for an easy to use way to grab screenshots? I use free software called Jing. http://www.techsmith.com/jing.html This makes it very easy to save examples of sites you like for future review. Be sure to type in the web address of each screen shot so you can find the website in the future.

EXAMPLE OF A GOOD WEBSITE

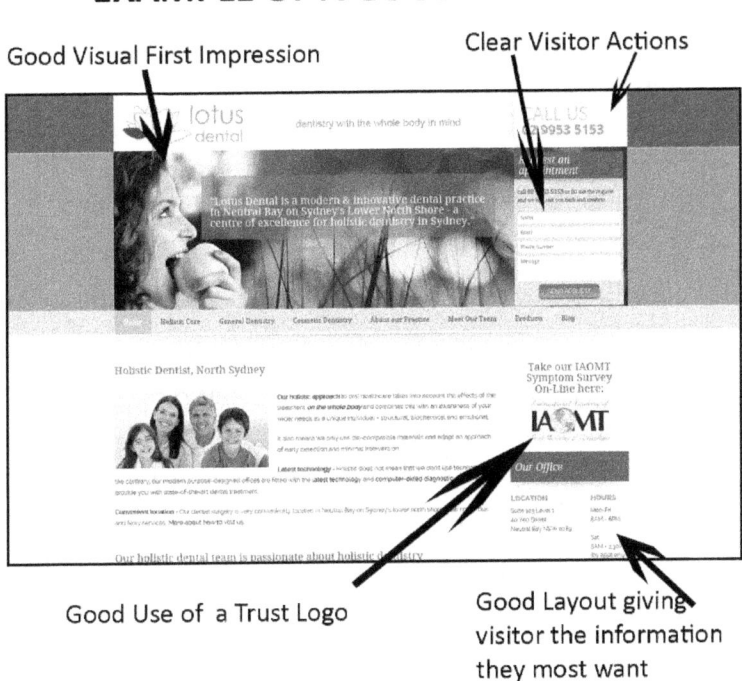

Good Visual First Impression

Clear Visitor Actions

Good Use of a Trust Logo

Good Layout giving visitor the information they most want

Figure 5.1 http://www.lotusdental.com.au

Further Analysis

If you end up saving 10-15 "good" websites that you like the layout on, then you will have enough of a pool to select your top 3-5 reference websites.

The easiest way to make your selections is to rate each website on how well you like them for each of the three categories. I will rate them 1-10 with ten being best. See the example rating sheet.

Website URL	First Impression	Good Layout	Clear CTA	Total Score
lotusdental.com.au	10	9	10	29
lighthousedental.net	6	7	7	20
mitchmarderdds.com	7	5	8	20

You will also want to take notes on your favorite 3-5 websites and what you like about them. This will help the designer when they create your design.

Below are typical comments when referring to a specific website. These are actual client comments taken from some of our past projects that we included to help the designers.

1. I like the colors, images and visual design great but it is a poor layout

2. I like the layout, simplicity and the overall design

3. I like how they did the buttons on right side

4. I hate the colors; I like the location of the call to action and layout

5. Visually poor and lacks organization. I do like how four problems are presented on the home page

6. I like the look of the website, clean, white look... but it is not designed well for conversion

7. Good organization, structure and layout. Professional graphic design

8. I like how video was included in rotating banner

Select one website that you liked the layout of. This can become the basis of planning your layout. Remember the layout is how the elements are arranged not the visual design i.e. colors. By elements we mean things such as navigation, top banner image, call to actions, how the text is organized into boxes, where videos are placed, etc.

If you narrow it down to two websites and know exactly how you'd combine them for your layout; create a rough sketch.

Functions and Features

As you look at competitor websites, identify features that you like and want to include on your website. Some common ones include-

1. Rotating top banner (commonly called a slider).

2. Ability to add videos into top slider

3. Photo gallery for Before and After

4. Email capture forms with autoresponder.

5. Email capture forms integrated to email system such as Mailchimp, Aweber or Constant Contact. Use on newsletter subscriptions, etc.

6. CAPTCHA added to forms. A CAPTCHA helps prevent spam submitted by robots. It is a series of numbers or letters filled in before submitting a web form.

7. Knowledgebase instead of a traditional FAQ page

8. eCommerce store

9. Surveys or polls

10. Google Maps and driving directions

Identify the functions and features that you want to include in your website.

The review you just completed compared the look and feel, call to actions and the features to include in your website.

———————

You can get the best ideas of what to include in your website by studying your competition. You can get ideas for designs, layouts, calls-to-actions, offers, functionality and why they are attracting traffic.

6 The Design Brief

You will want to gather all of your plans for your new website into a single document called the design brief. Building this design brief allows you to consider and plan all the key elements for your website.

This also serves as a set of instructions for your web development team making sure they will be able to produce the website that your practice needs. This helps focus their creativity.

The Design Brief

The format can differ, but the key elements remain the same. This is the design brief format that we use in planning websites for our clients.

Prepare a formal written document that includes-

1. **Domain and Website Logins**. This will give the developers the access to the current site and to make the new website live.

    a. Website URL

    b. Domain Registrar and domain login

    c. Current website FTP and admin panel login

    d. Google Analytics and Webmaster Tools logins

2. **Description and Objectives**- These items form a summary of the project. Each item should only be about one paragraph in length.

   a. Business Description- What services or products does the practice provide, positioning, major marketing initiatives and 2 year goals.

   b. Project Description- Describe any special functionality, custom programming or data importing that must be done as part of the project.

   c. Website Objectives- What business results do you expect from the website? List in priority order if more than one.

   d. Mobile- How important is mobile? What actions or content are important for mobile? i.e. phone number should be clickable to place call.

3. **Targeted Audience**. If you have more than one patient profile, list your best. Most sought after patient first. Should be one paragraph per patient profile and include buying triggers.

   Your targeted patient will drive call to actions and even design. A design for 60 year olds needs to be visually simple with larger fonts. Why? Because they have weaker eyes and can't read low contrast or smaller fonts.

4. **Design Information**

    a. Design objectives- Any design boundaries or is a specific look wanted? i.e. Large format graphics

    b. Colors- List any colors that are part of branding. Are there colors that you definitely want or colors that must be avoided? If you have a specific color, specify the HTML color number or take a screen shot of the color on a website.

    c. Logo- Provide the designer a high resolution copy of the logo. Will a tagline or slogan be used?

    d. Provide a list of 3-5 reference websites. Describe what specifically you like about each. This gives the designer insight into what you like.

    e. Interior page designs- How many separate interior page design layouts do you want? Typical is one.

    f. Landing page- Will landing pages be wanted for PPC campaigns?

5. **Conversion** - These are your plans to reassure and get visitors to take action.

    a. Trust elements- Describe strategies to build trust with the visitor. This would include trust logos.

Privacy and returns policies, customer reviews, etc

b. Social Media link locations- Which social media icons to include? The most common ones are Google+, Twitter, Facebook, YouTube, Pinterest, LinkedIn

c. Call-to-actions- Provide a prioritized list from the most important to the least important

d. Provide a list of videos that will be used along with a link to where they are hosted. i.e. YouTube or Vimeo

e. Is there a free report or eBook that will be offered as part of your email list building?

f. Email list- Will emails collected need to be added to an existing list? If so, where is this list maintained?

g. eCommerce? Will there be online product or service sales? How will payments be taken?

6. **Content writing**- Who will be writing the content for the website? You can write it yourself or hire a professional writer. Don't expect a web developer to write for you. Someone who is a marketer should do the writing. The developer will need the content before they create the design to incorporate it into the design layout.

a. Web pages

    b. Landing pages

    c. Auto responder emails.

    d. Email drip campaign emails.

7. Sitemap and SEO Plan

A sitemap is a list of the pages and subpages to be included in your website. It shows how they relate to each other.

The flow of your website should follow your natural selling process. When you design your website structure, begin by thinking like a customer.

This is actually "story-boarding" your sales presentation. Having a picture of your whole web site will make it easier to create a menu system that is useful to your visitors.

Dr. Jones has a pediatric dental practice located in Denver. He and his office manager were planning their new website. They started out by listing out the topics that parents of their new patients would want to know.

    a. Available dental services
    b. Info about the doctor
    c. Is office clean and orderly?
    d. What are their office hours?
    e. What is the office location?
    f. What insurances do they take?
    g. How to make an appointment

This is a simple site map that would answer these questions. The typical dental website is often large at 50+ pages.

Level		Page
1		Home page
1		Services
	2	Preventive Care
	2	Laser Dentistry
	2	Orthodontics
1		Our Practice
	2	Dr. Jones
	2	Office Tour (photos)
	2	Hours & Directions
	2	Insurance & Financial
1		Make an Appointment
	2	New Patient Forms
	2	Hours & Directions
1		Reviews

Figure 6.1 Example of a Sitemap

Guidelines for creating a sitemap

1. Start by listing out the pages to include. Avoid using obscure names for your pages; it will only confuse your visitors. Your Home Page should explain what you provide and why they should choose you. The About Us page should talk about your history, mission, vision and values.

2. Primary pages to be included in the main navigation are listed with a "1". Subpages may be a "2" or "3".

3. Group pages that cover the same general topic. Then order them according to how people will look for them. For example, people will first look for information about the services provided and then want to learn about the practice before requesting an appointment. Reviews were added to be on the end of the navigation to make them more visible and to reassure with social proof.

4. It is OK to list the same page under more than one category. We did that with the Hours & Directions page since it applies to both the practice and appointment categories.

5. The sequence of topics should match your best sales process. The sitemap above is sequenced to follow the selling sequence for this practice. You will want to design this around your practice.

Once you have a listing of pages, use the keywords from your research and match with the most relevant phrases for each page. Start by focusing on one primary keyword phrase per page. This will serve as a guide for your content writing.

Dental practices are searched for by location so include the city in the keywords. City is more often searched by being placed after the keyword phrase.

If we look at our example: Denver dentist is searched for 19 times per day and dentist Denver is searched 43 times per day. So in this example more than 2X search with the city following the keyword.

Level		Page	Primary Keyword Phrase
1		Home page	pediatric dentist denver
1		Services	dental care services denver
	2	Preventive Care	dental clinic denver
	2	Laser Dentistry	laser dentistry denver
	2	Orthodontics	orthodontics denver
1		Dentist Office	pediatric dentist office denver
	2	Dr. Jones	denver pediatric dentist
	2	Office Tour (photos)	denver dental office
	2	Hours & Directions	pediatric dental office hours
	2	Insurance & Financial	dental insurance denver
1		Make an Appointment	pediatric dental appointment
	2	New Patient Forms	pediatric dentist forms
	2	Hours & Directions	
1		Reviews	reviews pediatric dentist denver

Figure 6.2 Example of a Sitemap with keyword phrase selected

SEO Plan

To create the full SEO plan, you will need to expand the sitemap example above. This will give the instructions the web developer needs to apply the important META tags to each web page.

1. Level (already on sitemap)
2. Page name to display on the menu (already on sitemap)
3. Primary keyword phrase (already on sitemap)
4. Secondary keyword
5. Title Tag
6. META Description
7. H1 Tag (main page headlines)

Details for how to create Title tags, META Description and H1 tags are discussed in Chapter 10 under the organic SEO section.

8. Wireframe (Last section of Design Brief)

A website wireframe is a schematic view of your web page layout. This is kind of a "first draft" used in planning and organizing a web page. It is a skeletal rendering of how the web page elements fit together onto the page.

Wireframing is generally done with grayscale block diagrams that illustrate the overall navigation and blocks of elements such as images, content and functionality. The call-to-actions are strategically located. These are organizational plans and not a completed design. They are done before any artwork is generated.

The term "wireframe" comes from the world of computer graphics and 3D animation. Here wireframes are used for prototyping and because they are quick to generate and they use a minimum of computer processing.

Wireframes can be created with many different computer programs. It does not require special software. I typically use Photoshop, but I have seen wireframes created in many different graphics programs. I have seen standard office programs such as Excel or Word. What are important are the positions of the key elements.

Using a planning wireframe will often generate new requirements and questions that hadn't been thought of before. It forces you to think through your website's functionality at the page level. Creating a sitemap and wireframe are essential steps before doing a website design.

1. Determine the basic layout such as how many columns the page will have. Should the navigation be along the top (horizontal) or on the side (vertical)?

2. Decide on the call to action for the page. Place it where it can be easily seen, preferably above the fold so it can be seen immediately by an arriving visitor without scrolling down.

3. Organize and place the page elements such as the header, footer, navigation, content objects, and branding elements. Group and prioritize the elements according to how you want them seen.

4. Label the navigation links, headings and content objects.

5. Use placeholders for text and images. Use dummy text such as lorem ipsum to show text areas.

The wireframe gives your web designer a visual guide to layout. This ensures the call to action and priority elements are placed on the page for maximum effectiveness.

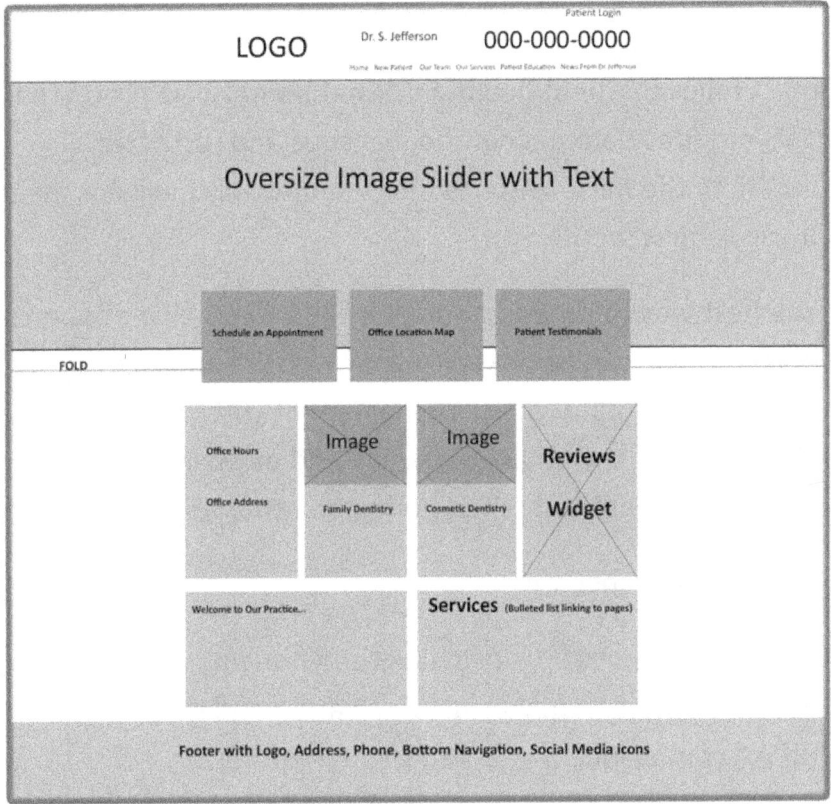

Figure 6.3 Example of a Wireframe

HIPAA Requirements

HIPAA compliance is one of the most important challenges a dental practice will face. How will HIPAA regulations affect what you can and cannot do with your website?

HIPAA is a law that makes many recommendations (addressable items) and a few requirements (required items). So in many cases it will be up to each practice to determine what they need to do to be compliant.

There are some minimum requirements that a website must follow. Patient health information must be protected. This requires data encryption, backups and restricted access to the data. Websites for the most part will not meet these requirements.

The best way to do this is to get a HIPAA-compliant patient portal. These can be linked to your website and can be integrated dental practice management software. This gives patients the ability to review and pay bills online, view their treatments and scheduled appointments.

HIPAA compliance tips

Patient Portal: Adding login links on your website gives patients access to powerful information and still maintains HIPAA compliance.

HIPAA notice: There is a federal requirement that dentists should post their HIPAA privacy practices onto their website.

Testimonials: Get signed HIPAA compliant releases from your patients before using their testimonials in marketing your practice.

Dental Forms: You should post your printable dental forms on your website to allow patients to fill them out at home and bring them to your office. There are also online services that allow patients to fill out your forms online and store their information on secure storage servers. You can provide links to these forms on your website.

Appointment Requests: It is common to allow patients to request appointments using web forms on the website. These forms and the emails that transmit the requests are generally not secure and encrypted. This means these appointment requests should not allow patients to enter patient health information. This means avoiding the use of a comments field in the form.

Decide how HIPAA rules will impact your website and build that into your design brief.

_____

Design Brief Outline

1. *Domain and Website Logins*
2. *Description and Objectives*
3. *Targeted Audience*
4. *Design Information*
5. *Conversion*
6. *Content writing*
7. *Sitemap and SEO Plan*
8. *Wireframe*

7 Crafting Your Message

The content on the typical business website is written to sell and promote. Some make use of use of hype, high pressure and the "hard sell." The writing for a medical or dental website should be designed to educate. This is an important difference.

Instead your approach needs to be that of education based marketing where your objective is to teach and provide valuable information to create trust and credibility.

Your website needs to be an extension of how you treat and talk to patients in your practice. In this chapter we will discuss how writing for web content is different. We will go through how and what to write for the different pages and sections of your website.

Web content needs to be different

Writing for the web is different than writing for print. You will want to write content for your website that is brief and to the point with shorter paragraphs, shorter sentences and fewer words, than a printed version.

People will read something more completely when it is written on paper and only skim information that is presented on the screen. They tend to ignore details, reading short paragraphs, headlines or bulleted lists.

Example: The paragraph on the prior page rewritten for the web.

People only skim info on the screen

- They ignore details

- Only read short paragraphs

- Read headlines

- Read bulleted lists

Why? They are able to read a paper document 25% faster. It is physically harder to read from the screen. It is harder on the eyes. There are a lot of reasons for this such as sharpness of font, font size, contrast, position of the screen.

In print you can control the reader from introduction to conclusion. With web content the visitor is in control and they choose their own path of what to read next. They follow navigation and links according to what interests them.

On the screen, few people read everything on a page. Most will scan a page looking for the information they are after. They skip whole blocks of text, particularly longer paragraphs.

The same way a graphic designer will call attention to elements with color, a web copywriter highlights with format and structure. This means headlines, using **bold**, bulleted lists, etc. Information in larger paragraphs is more hidden.

8 content writing tips

1. It's about them- Spend less time writing about your practice and answer how you will solve their problem. Remember, your primary duty is to give them what they need.

2. Back up what you say- Web visitors don't believe hype. If you want to be believable, you have to back it up. Reference your sources.

3. 3 Second Rule- Internet users are active, not passive. If they don't immediately see what they are looking for, they are gone within 3 seconds. First impressions are critical.

4. Be brief- Use shorter sentences, words and paragraphs. Use one idea per paragraph and use about half the words than you would use in writing for print.

5. Active Voice- Write concisely, plainly and openly. Write using action oriented words to get your message across as quickly as possible. Don't be elusive or try to reach everyone. Instead of saying, "Our service will help you

be more effective in your personal dental care." Try saying, "We teach how to prevent cavities."

 Make your content easy and quick to digest. Write your content so it can be understood by a third grade reading level. You are writing to be understood, not to impress.

6. Start strong and finish strong- Grab their attention when they arrive, and astound them with your finish. Put your best material at the beginning and the end.

7. Easy to scan- Your reader wants to scan down your web page and get the gist of it before reading. The main points should stand out in sub-headlines, lists, images, colors, italics and indented text.

8. Action- Each page should guide your visitor into taking action. Your visitor arrives ready to take action. Tell them what to do. "To schedule a consultation with Dr.XXXX , or to learn more about XXXXXXX contact our dental office today at (XXX) XXX-XXXX.

Good content writing entertains, educates and convinces your audience. By skillfully weaving in keywords, content writing also gets the attention of the search engines.

Writing for SEO

You want your website to be found when people do a Google search. You do this by incorporating keywords into each page of your website. You will use the sitemap – SEO plan that you prepared in the last chapter.

SEO is about optimizing a website for people that use search engines. This is this human side of search engine optimization. Use keywords as a central theme in your messaging, your page headlines and your hyperlinks. It is about establishing relevance to what your visitors are searching for.

Targeted keyword phrases are woven into marketing text so search engines take note of the important phrases. Your writing must be convincing to both website visitors and the search engines.

Your page headline should grab your reader's attention and contain keywords. Body text should stimulate interest and assure your reader they are in the right place. Are you clearly addressing the *burning question* that your ideal buyer will have? Write in a customer focused style.

Your most important keyword phrase should be used a minimum of 3 times.

1. Once in the main headline (H1)

2. Once in the first paragraph

3. Once in text that will be hyperlinked to another relevant page on your site

If you have a secondary keyword, it should be used 1-2 times.

Try and use your keywords in the beginning of the page headline. The keywords that you are targeting should appear at the beginning of your page, beginning of your paragraphs and even the beginning of your sentences. These first words are given more importance by the search engines.

Emphasize keyword phrases by putting them in **bold**, *italics* and bulleted lists.

An optimized web page should have a minimum of 300 words of text. 400 is better. Break up your content into small articles for easy reading the way a newspaper does.

The ABCs of writing your home page

The Home Page is the most important page in your website. It is the page that first greets visitors. A visitor will spend only seconds scanning your Home Page and then decide to either enter your site or leave. Your Home Page is also the most valued page by the search engines as they look for keywords.

A visitor comes to your site with an assortment of questions, but they all boil down to- "Can you help me with my problem?" This means when writing to your customer, you need to address *their* concerns and talk about solutions, not your product or service.

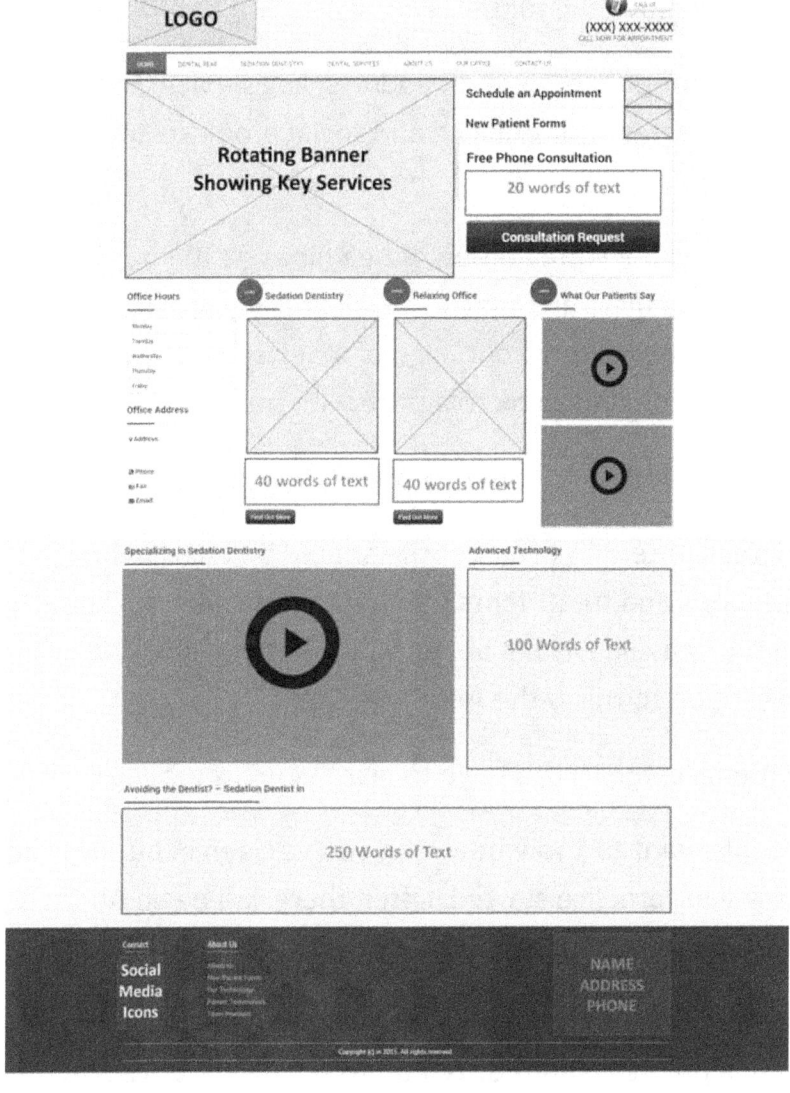

Figure 7.1 Home Page Wireframe example

Above the fold refers to the area of the page that is visible without scrolling down. Studies have shown that a high percent of your visitors will never read the content at the bottom of the page. You need to place your most important content above the fold.

Show your phone number, address, key services, what differentiates your practice and social proof (reviews / testimonials) in this above the fold area.

Do this with a combination of headlines, text, images, graphic banners and maybe a welcome video. Write your home page like the front page of a newspaper with a short introduction and a link to a page with more details.

The trust building About Us page

All the content in your website should be focused on solutions and treatments for your dental patients. You carefully avoid writing about how great you are. The exception to this is the About Us page.

Patients come to this page to learn your story.

People want to know how long you've been in business and how your practice started. Often there will be an About us page and a separate meet the doctor page.

Visitors will also look to see if you are a real dental office with a physical address. Tell them a little about your practice instead of the long history.

This is your chance to cement a relationship and connect with someone who is curious about you. Describe how you are different and better than other dental office. Share your dental care philosophies, awards and certifications. If you have important affiliations, this is the page to include them.

The About Us page should be concise and easy to read. Its main purpose is to build trust and credibility with your visitor. People want to feel safe and secure before they book an appointment.

Services, Treatment or Patient Education

These pages should be written to educate about a condition, treatment. It is OK to acknowledge that you provide this service and then go into a clear description of the condition and how it is treated. It is also OK to suggest at the conclusion that they contact your office for an appointment.

Do you have writers block?

Many doctors are great at talking with patients for endless hours. These same people suffer complete writers block when they sit down in front of a blank computer screen to write content for their website.

Start by jotting down a series of questions that need to be answered for each page of the website. Get someone to play the part of the patient and ask you these questions and record your conversation.

GoToMeeting.com or FreeConferenceCall.com allows you to record. You can use a transcription service to convert your words to text or send your recording to a professional writer to turn your words into your website.

This method captures your vision and passion for your business into your website. The challenge now becomes how to limit the volume of information to include onto each page.

Set up a writing schedule

Writing the content for your website can be an overwhelming project. This has been the biggest single delay in getting a website completed when business owners elect to write the content themselves.

If you are in doubt that you will have the time or the discipline to write the content for your website, then hire a professional writer.

Start with your home page. This is normally written as 4-6 short articles that introduce visitors to other areas of your website. (See the wireframe example).

The web designer will need this text as they design your website. Many designers can work knowing the headlines and how many words of text will be in each block.

The next page to write is the About Us page. This is usually an easier page to write. Each page you write will be easier than the page before.

Then setup a writing schedule such as 2-5 pages per week until the writing is complete.

Images and videos

Images should be used in every web page to add visual variety and to help communicate your ideas. Many people are visual learners and use of photos and graphics helps communicate your ideas.

Use photos you have taken, graphics you have had created or purchase royalty free stock images from services such as gettyimages.com or canstockphoto.com.

Warning- It is not OK to use a photo from another website without permission. It is NOT OK to modify a copyrighted image *and then call it your own. Modifying a work, say by cropping, coloring, distorting, enlarging, etc. is not a way around Copyright laws.*

It is OK to use someone's concept and create your own original image as long as no part of the original is directly copied. Merely using an original work as a model or inspiration does not by itself constitute an infringement.

Adding short videos to your website adds another dimension to your content. Videos catch a visitor's attention and persuade them to take action. They add a voice and a face to your website, helping brand you as the expert. Adding video is almost like sitting across the table from an interested prospect.

Most visitors will take the time to watch a video if the website seems relevant to their search. If you choose your videos well you will notice that people will stay on your website longer.

Web video is a powerful way to educate while allowing visitors to feel entertained. People learn in different ways and presenting only text may work well for search engines, but it limits your ability to interact with your audience. People today respond more to video than they do to text alone.

———————

The writing for a medical or dental website should be designed to educate. Your objective is to teach and provide valuable information to create trust and credibility.

Your website needs to be an extension of how you treat and talk to patients in your practice.

8 You Must Design For Mobile

A good mobile strategy is important for your practice. To plan your strategy you need to have a clear understanding of what your mobile visitors are looking for. The volume of mobile visitors has been growing quickly. But how significant is this to your dental practice?

One recent study places this at 29% for the average website (2014) with a rate of growth at 30% over 2013.[8] In this study mobile numbers included mobile phones and tablets.

Our dental clients are seeing 30-37% mobile visitors in the last half of 2015. This is steadily growing.

Let's look at some other recent mobile web statistics

In the US, 67% of mobile Internet users said they mostly or only used mobile, as opposed to the desktop, to go online and surf the web.[9]

45 percent of users between 18 and 29 use mobile search daily[10]

More than half (55%) of conversions from mobile search take place within the hour, while 81% of conversions occur within five hours.[11]

Mobile search is more common in the evenings, with 22% of searches taking place between 8pm and midnight.[11]

95% of mobile users use their devices for local search. [12]

52% of all local searches are done from a mobile device. [12]

What conclusions can you draw?

1. If you have a local business that caters to consumers like a dental or a medical office, then your website MUST be setup for mobile visitors.

2. If your website targets a younger demographic such as under 30, mobile will be even more important to you.

The mobile web

Mobile devices load websites more slowly than a desktop. They typically run on slower networks, mobile browsers parse and execute HTML more slowly. Mobile browser cache is smaller than desktop computers.

Page load time is critical for your mobile version of your website if you want your visitors to have a great user experience.

You get faster load times by using fewer graphics and the ones you do use must be reduced size graphics

Check your website to see how fast the page load speed is for both desktop and mobile by going to- http://developers.google.com/speed/pagespeed/insights/

Simpler- Look at ways to greatly simplify your design, your content and the number of pages. Focus your content on just what your mobile web visitor needs to know. You want the website to be easily read when it first loads without needing to zoom in.

The numbers and sizes of mobile displays continue to grow in number. Websites today need to display correctly on smartphones (portrait and landscape); mini tablets such as the iPad mini (portrait and landscape); full size tablets such as the standard iPad (portrait and landscape) and desktop displays.

Separate Mobile Websites

In the past, the solution was to build one or more mobile versions of your website. A switcher script "sensed" which display a visitor was using and then presented the correctly sized website. This is termed adaptive websites.

Usually simplified content was presented that was shorter and there were fewer pages. Typically there are just two versions; the desktop version and the smartphone version. Many sites are still using this system today.

See an example of a dental website using a separate mobile website in figure 8.1. The problem comes when someone tries to view the website on a mini tablet and gets a hard to look at website.

Mobile website is a separate website

Figure 8.1 Adaptive Websites

The advantage of a separate mobile website is that it can be added to a current website as an add-on. These separate mobile websites can be highly optimized for page load speed.

You have the option to have different amounts of content on different versions of the websites. You can have 25-50 word pages on your mobile version and 150 words per web page if you create a separate Kindle version. And 300 words of text on a Desktop version.

This means you can completely manage the user experience

The disadvantage is that a separate website must be built and maintained for each display you want to display correctly on. This can create a real headache and extra expense when you have to manage multiple versions of the same website.

Let's say you have a desktop and a smartphone version. What to you use on a mini tablet or a full size tablet? The trend is toward an increasing number of screen sizes as the line between smartphones, tablets and desktops continues to blur. Things were simpler when there were just smartphones.

Responsive Websites

Responsive websites have the ability to detect the viewer's screen size and serve up appropriately organized text and graphics that are properly sized to ensure the best possible viewing experience.

With a responsive web design you don't have a separate mobile website. Instead you have one website that responds, re-sizes and reconfigures itself according to the viewing screen. This seems to be where the future and the direction web design and websites are headed. (See the example on the next page.)

One Website Fits All Devices

Figure 8.2 Responsive Websites

The advantage is that they are easier to deploy and maintain a single website and the responsive technology takes care of the formatting which provides a website that can be viewed well from any possible device.

Disadvantages include slower page load times.

 Is your website responsive? Check for yourself by going to http://ami.responsivedesign.is/ and see what your website looks like. This is the way we created figure 8.2 above.

Which is better Responsive or Separate Mobile Websites?

So which is better for a small business? Our belief is that managing multiple website with the separate mobile websites is a cost and management time that most small businesses cannot afford.

Creating and managing separate versions of the same website can create a better visitor experience. Whether it's worth that extra expense is something each business needs to answer based on their priorities.

You might ask which works better for SEO with Google. They support either approach and this should not affect your decision. Google does not favor any particular URL format as long as they are all accessible for all Googlebots.[13]

Plan for your mobile visitor first

When you design using responsive web design, start by first considering the mobile visitor instead of the desktop visitor. This is a complete paradigm shift from our past.

By planning what your priorities are for your mobile visitor first, your design can be integrated into your desktop design.

This could be click to call on phone numbers, click to map on addresses, prioritizing the content to what mobile visitors are most interested in.

Low priority content can be hidden that can be accessed with a click.

———————————

The older technology uses separate versions of your website. A switcher script "senses" which display type a visitor has and then presents the correctly sized website.

The newer technology is called responsive. Responsive websites have the ability to detect the viewer's screen size and serve up appropriately organized text and graphics that are properly sized to ensure the best possible viewing experience. This is all based on a single website.

9   Getting Your Website Built

Custom vs. templated dental websites

You have the choice between getting a templated dental website that is formatted and comes complete with stock content that is quick to deploy.

Your other option is to get a fully custom website that is custom built for your practice.

Often new practices will elect to get a standard dental website which is usually has several design options, stock prewritten content and these are usually priced very reasonably since the same website can be used for hundreds of dental offices and the development cost is spread over a large base.

Although quick to deploy and low cost is attractive, there is a down side. You have limited ability to configure call to actions, branding is not customized to your practice and most important, the stock content is a huge problem with the search engines.

This stock content is viewed as duplicate content by Google and Bing. This means your website will either be ignored or worse yet penalized for this duplicate content.

This is why most mature practices will opt to have a fully custom dental website so they can be a powerhouse in attracting local search traffic.

New practices need to weigh the pros and cons of a custom website based on financial cost vs better performance. If you elect to go with a templated solution, you can skip the remainder of this chapter.

If you are moving ahead with a custom designed website, please read on.

High Performance Custom Dental Websites

You are now ready to get your website built. Up until now you have been planning how your website will market for your practice. Now it is time to bring in the technical experts that will design and code your new website.

In this chapter we will talk about how to select a web development firm, the typical website building process and the final QA check that you need to be run before your new site goes live.

Roles of the website project team

Before you outsource the website, you need to assess the skills and strengths of your project team.

You have the sole responsibility of getting the website built. You need to make sure these roles are being filled with either internal team members or are being outsourced. This team may or may not already exist on the same team as the web developer. Often your content writers and web strategist are hired separately. Larger web companies or agencies will have people that will fill these roles for you.

Project Manager- They keep the project on track and on schedule. They have the overall responsibility for the successful planning, execution, monitoring and control of the project. They manage all the moving parts and continually steer the team toward completing the website. Without a good project manager, website projects always seem to stall.

Strategist- This person plans the purpose of the website, what products and services are being marketed to the target audience, and how the buying decision is made. They compare the competition and craft the central message for the website. They establish the goals for the website, call to actions on the website.

SEO Specialist- Your website needs to attract interested visitors. A skilled search engine optimization person will pick the right keywords, advise on website structure, do page optimization, establish link popularity strategies and set-up metrics to measure success. The SEO person will work closely with the content writer.

Site Architect- They organize and categorize the website structure and content. They create the sitemap and wireframes. They work with the strategist to organize the pages into a selling sequence. They are responsible for usability and shape the user experience as they interact with the website.

Figure 9.1 Anatomy of a Website Project

Content Writer- The writer is responsible for creating all the website content. The writer takes the message and crafts interesting and exciting text, weaving in the keywords keeping the audience and search engines interested in the website. Creative writing will create the emotional spark that causes visitors to take action.

Graphic Designer- The designer is responsible for the visual appearance with designs that encourage visitors to take action. The design establishes trust and credibility and is more than just "pretty." A good designer is an artist, understands visitor interaction and is a good marketer. They will design for usability to insure a good visitor experience. Sometimes the usability expert will be a separate role in major websites.

Developer / Programmer- This person codes the website and adds the interaction functionality to the website. They turn designs into an interactive user experience. Programmers add custom database applications programs that allow your site to sell products and interact with the web visitor.

Many times one person on the team will fill multiple positions. For very complex projects, each role may be filled by a team of specialists. Imagine the size of the team needed to construct and maintain a major website like Amazon.com or Facebook.com.

Projects can often be greatly simplified by using a standard platform such as WordPress that can still be 100% customized to deliver any visual appearance and special functions that you may need. WordPress websites are less complex to maintain and are usually less expensive.

Before hiring a web developer, take an inventory of the skill sets that exist in your project team and where you need outside expertise. This will help you decide what skills the web developer needs to bring to the project.

Selecting a developer

Here are things to look at when you hire a web designer.

1. **Do they understand your goals?** Your website needs to meet your business objective which is why you prepared your design brief. Do they understand your goals and how they will implement them? Do they example of similar websites that they have designed and built?

2. **Which platform do they specialize in?** This is the content management / website management system used to build your website on. WordPress is the most common one in use today and is easy to take your website to another web company if you have to. Stay away from proprietary systems that don't give you the portability in case you need to move it.

   Let me give you an example of a proprietary platform. When I had my own web design firm, we developed our own content management system that allowed us to quickly deploy photo galleries, blogs and all sorts of great functionality on websites we built. The downside was it was our system and other developers couldn't easily work on the system.

Today, I strongly recommend WordPress. This is the most popular platform in the world. It is extremely easy to find someone to work on your WordPress website.

3. **How do they design for mobile?** Do they offer responsive web design? Look at examples of their sites on your phone and tablet. Make sure their skills will match you mobile objectives.

4. **Do they understand how to design for web traffic?** Organic search rankings are important. Make sure to choose a designer experienced in SEO. They should be able to demonstrate SEO results. Search Engine Optimization should be designed in with keywords built into navigation, page names, links and body text.

5. **Can they integrate web applications?** Most websites today includes web applications. By adding online tools, searchable databases of your work, pricing wizards, shopping carts and complex sign-up applications you can automate your business website. These can be programmed from scratch or be easily integrated with plugins which is a WordPress term.

6. **Who will maintain the website?** Once the website is complete, who will maintain the website? Website maintenance includes changing content, photos, adding pages, adding applications or adding a blog. If something breaks, who will fix it?

7. **Who will host the website?** It is nice to have one source for your web needs. Make sure you are getting high quality business website hosting that is maintained within a data center. One that has multiple Internet trunks and power backups. Stay away from designers who host on a computer in their office or apartment.

Other things to look for: What is their lead time? Will they supply a written fixed price proposal? How long have they been in business? Will they still be in business when you need help? Are they easy to reach and communicate with?

It will really come down to who are you the most comfortable in working with. Which firm will most likely deliver a website that will get you the results you need.

A website that doesn't deliver results is just an expense. A website that delivers leads or online sales is an effective marketing tool that generates revenue.

Typical Website Development Process

Each company may vary slightly in how they build out your website, but this is the typical process that most established firms follow.

1. **Information gathering-** Much of this information will already be in the design brief you created. Includes the project definition, deliverables, your design preferences,

home page layout, sitemap, gathering logins, sources for images, videos and web content.

2. **Design concept-** If you have not prepared the wireframe for the home page, this will be their first step. Then one or more design concepts are done and submitted to you for approval. These are designed in a graphics program such as Photoshop or similar program. Changes are easy to make.

3. **Website Development-** Once there are approved design concepts for the home and interior pages, the design is "sliced" and coded into the platform such as WordPress. Navigation is created and blank pages created. This is the backbone for the new website. Website functionality such as blog, photo galleries, events calendars and ecommerce are added.

4. **Page Population-** The text content, images and videos are added to the website. They are arranged on the pages to make them visually appealing. SEO is applied using the SEO plan that you prepared. If you have an ecommerce shopping cart, the products must be either manually copied over or imported into the new shopping cart.

5. **Testing and Final QA-** The developer will go through and test to make sure all of the functions on the website work correctly, the ages display correctly in the most

popular browsers and on mobile displays. The website is checked for broken links, etc.

6. **Acceptance-** The client tests the website and verifies everything is working correctly and buys off on the website. The next section provides some guidelines and tools for your testing. You will want to prepare final list of items to fix before you accept the website.

7. **GoLive and Training-** This is the cutover to make the website live. Check to make sure emails and web forms work correctly. Do an actual transaction if your site includes ecommerce and make sure payments are received. Verify 301 redirects have been created to make sure you don't lose your current search rankings.

   Training is normally provided on using your new website. Sometimes this is done with instructional videos.

How to Quality Check Your New Website

When you are asked to buy off on your website before going live, what should you be checking for? Here are a series of visual checks and free web tools to do your own quality check.

These tests cover the basics. There are an almost overwhelming number of tools and tests that could be run. The key is to quickly uncover the major issues before you take possession of your new site. Some of these tests may need to be run once your new website is live such as the www vs. non-www check.

1. Visual checks- Go through each page on your website to make sure it displays correctly. You should check using the latest version of each major browser.

    As of the writing of this book (January 2016), Chrome had a 67% browser market share, followed by Firefox with 19%. Check current browser market shares at- http://www.w3schools.com/browsers/browsers_stats.asp

    An easy way to check a page using multiple browsers is with https://browsershots.org/

    Test your website on your mobile phone and on an iPad. You can also use an emulator that will show how your website looks on many different display types. http://deviceponsive.com/ or http://ami.responsivedesign.is/

2. Manually test every function. Buy something from your store and sign-up for your newsletter. Do you receive all the proper email notifications? Are the email notifications formatted and worded correctly.

3. www vs. non-www- Your website should show a redirect to either the www or non-www version of your

site. Do this by trying to manually switch from www.yourdomain.com to http://yourdomain.com. Does automatically switch back to the version you want?

4. Broken Links- Check all internal and external links using a broken link checker. Two free checkers that you can download and install on your computer for doing this are-

    Screaming Frog SEO Spider http://www.screamingfrog.co.uk/seo-spider/

    Xenu's Link Sleuth http://xenus-link-sleuth.en.softonic.com/

5. HTML Code Validation- Verify your pages were built within coding standards. Validate all HTML code with W3C Validation. This helps with cross browser compatibility. http://validator.w3.org/

 Do a free Website Review - Looking for a system that will perform a whole range of checks (not the visual or manual testing)? Try www.woorank.com. You can sign up for a free 14 day trial

301 redirects to prevent loss of search rankings

Many times new websites have completely new page URLs. You may be switching from pages that end in .html to pages that end in PHP. The trouble with this is you will instantly lose your search engine traffic to these pages as the search engines detect the old pages are gone. Instead put in place 301 redirects to redirect traffic to the new pages.

This can be done through your web developer where they do this in the HTaccess file. This can easily be done in Wordpress websites using a plugin called Redirection to manage 301 redirects and detect 404 errors.

———————————

Often new practices will elect to get a templated dental website which is usually has several design options, stock prewritten content and these are usually priced very reasonably since the same website can be used for hundreds of dental offices and the development cost is spread over a large base.

New practices need to weigh the pros and cons of a custom website based on financial cost vs better performance.

10   Increase Website Traffic

Your objective is to bring in more new patients. Your dental website will be the hub that all your marketing will send visitors to. Visitors may find your website through a Google search or they may be a referral from a patient and they will check out your website before giving you a call.

Visitor traffic should come to your website from multiple sources including digital and traditional marketing campaigns. Be prepared to continually look at ways to promote your dental practice.

Be creative and always be looking for ways to reach prospective patients.

20 ways to drive website traffic

1. Organic SEO- Organic SEO means getting your website listed in the natural search results (not the paid ads). This should be your backbone strategy that attracts your best patients as they search your local area on Google and other search engines.

2. Google My Business Listings- These local business listings appear near the top on Google searches as a separate group of listings or as part of their map listings. This is free and does require that your business has a website.

3. Pay Per Click- Advertise directly on the search engines to get almost instant results. Typically dental practices do best when they send traffic to a relevant page on their website or create microsites instead of landing pages.

4. Retargeting or remarketing- This is a type of pay per click advertising that will display ads only to people that have already visited your website. When someone visits your website, cookies are then placed on their browser, and as they browse around the web, your ads will appear to them. This is low cost and very effective.

5. Social Media- This includes blog marketing, social networking and more. You can set up profiles on popular social networking sites like Facebook.

6. New Patient Offer: Create a compelling offer for new patients such as a $50 gift card. Promote this on social media, your blog, in Google AdWords, via direct mail and on your website.

7. Develop online coupon specials and promote these in the same ways you would promote the new patient offer.

8. Patient Referrals- This is usually the best single source of new patients for your practice. Often 70-80% of new patients will come from referrals from existing patients.

Asking for referrals is natural when patients are near the end of a successful treatment.

9. Web Directories- Submitting your site to local directories is still a valid and cost effective link building method that should be part of developing your portfolio of back links. Select directories that people will actually use; there are many low quality directories. The single best directory to submit to is Dmoz.org (and it's free).

10. Post Educational Articles- Write and publish educational articles and place them on article syndication sites. Articles should be original and interesting to be successful. The articles have to be good quality.

11. Start a blog- Add a blog to your website and post at least monthly. Weekly is even better. Each blog posting adds one new page of keyword rich content to your website. Content growth is an important part of SEO with the Google algorithm.

12. Become guest author- Write postings on other blogs. Many of the major blogs are on the lookout for quality fresh content for their site.

13. Email marketing- Develop regular emails that go to your patient base providing weekly dental tips and dental fun facts.

14. Dental Patient Referrers like 1-800-DENTIST can be a steady source of new patients.

15. Rave reviews on Google+ and Yelp helps boost your credibility and brings in new patients. Encourage patients to leave reviews helps increase your number of reviews. There are services that will help with the encouraging patients to leave reviews.

16. Direct mail postcards. The post office Every Door Direct Mail allows you to inexpensively deliver to every household in an area. There are also ways to target mail to people just moving into the area.

17. Traditional Print advertising in local newspapers and circulars. Include your URL on all newspaper and magazine ads. Do advertising in local neighborhood directories that are close to your office location.

18. Local Press – do something newsworthy that will get the attention of a local news.

19. Networking – Get out in your community either by volunteering or participating in your local chamber or other networking groups. You can also sponsor a little league or soccer team.

20. Traditional Marketing- Drive traffic to your site by including your website URL in all your other marketing methods such as business cards, brochures, flyers, email

signatures, radio and TV ads, direct mail, etc. You get more results when you get all your marketing methods to work together.

Organic Search Engine Optimization

Organic SEO means getting your website listed in the natural search results (not the paid ads). Google is the most important search engine to focus on since they have the largest market share of searches. Bing and Yahoo combined are only about 22%.[14]

The first step in SEO is selecting your keyword phrases. Not just any keywords, you need keyword phrases that attract patients.

When people begin researching online they start with short, very general phrases. They may search for Denver dentist. As they go along, they continually get more specific and keep adding words to their searches. By the time they want to select a dentist their search will be for Commerce City pediatric dentist.

The final search phrases are often very specific and will include specific requirements or specific locations.

More specific keyword phrases almost always have fewer competitors and it is much faster to get top rankings.

In many cases, you can't plan for every possible search phrase. But then you really don't have to. If you have a large website, with many pages of keyword rich content, Google will index all that content. If someone does a highly specific search and that comes close to matching your web content, then your website will be served up in the search results.

This is where it is very important to have original content on your website. If you use stock content which is typically patient education content that comes from a standardized library. This same content is usually served up on dozens if not hundreds of other dental websites.

Google is very good at identifying duplicate content and for the most part ignores these pages that are duplicated across the web.

SEO Plan

In Chapter 6, you created your sitemap and SEO Plan so the developer could build the SEO into your website. Your SEO plan should include the following-

1. Navigation Level (see Ch 6)
2. Page name to display on the menu (see Ch 6)
3. Primary keyword phrase (see Ch 6))
4. Secondary keyword
5. Title Tag
6. META Description
7. H1 Tag (main page headlines)

Each page of the website will need a primary keyword and a secondary keyword. The primary keyword is the primary focus of the web page. Choose a secondary keyword that will be used in the content writing, just to a lesser extent.

If the website is a local business, the secondary phrase should be the City, State to help apply local SEO.

Local SEO for the Dental Practice

If your practice has a single office location, applying local SEO is pretty straight forward. Each page of your website should include your address, city and state. The easiest way to do this is to include your office address on every page.

In your page content, use your local community name either just before or just after your primary keyword for that page. It is the combination of your community name and the keyword that make up your local keyword phrase.

A common question is "how important is it the order of the words?" People search most often with the keyword followed by the community name. But they also search with the city before the keyword, just not quite as often. So it is more important that your sentences sound natural than trying to artificially get the order correct.

For local SEO, use the community name (usually city) and the primary keyword in the Title Tag, Description Tag and the H1 tag. Use the keyword and community name in the content a few times.

Multi Office SEO: If your practice has multiple offices, then you will want to create at least one page per location. Creating a cluster of pages for each location is even more powerful.

For each office location you should write about things your patients want to know. This can be location, hours, services offered, short bios on team members. You get the idea.

Think of each location as a small focused microsite within your main website. Google places more importance and rewards with better rankings if you have well optimized groups of pages for each location.

Title Tag Best Practices

The Title Tag describes a webpage for both search engines and for visitors. It is the single most important SEO element for page level SEO (on-page factors). Many times simply fixing Title Tags alone will improve search engine rankings for a website.

It not only appears visibly at the top of your browser, it appears in the HTML code of your website and as the main headline in the search engine results page (SERP).

A well-crafted title tag will help get a top ranking and catch the attention of a searcher to begin the conversion process by inviting them to your web page. It should be an accurate, concise description of the content on the web page.

Title Tag format- Keyword 1, Keyword 2 | Company (or brand) name

Your Title Tag should be unique (not duplicated on other pages). It should contain the central topic of the web page. Words placed at the beginning of the Title Tag are given more importance than the words at the end. This is why the most important keyword phrase for a web page should be at the beginning. The dental practice name is typically placed at the end.

If you have an Orthodontist in Los Angeles that wants to promote their Invisalign product, it might look like:

Los Angeles Orthodontist, Invisalign | Dr. Arlene Novick

Optimal Title Tag length- 50-60 characters. The maximum is whatever will fit into a 512 pixel display which is 55-60 characters.

Local- Dental practices is looking for local patients so include city and or state. Typically people will search using the keyword + location or location + keyword.

Compelling- Your Title Tag will appear in the search results. Make it compelling so it will pull in more visits from the search results.

Unique- Each page should have a unique Title Tag. Duplicate titles will harm search rankings.

META Description Tags Best Practices

META Description tags are not about SEO directly, but their message will attract guests to your website. Description Tags are used as the description in Google search results; so make them compelling. They should be unique and relevant for each page on your website.

On a search results page the Title Tag serves as the title for the search result. The META Description serves as the body. When no Description Tag exists, a snippet of relevant text is pulled from the page text.

Think of your Description Tag as a mini elevator pitch that is done in 160 characters or less. So its length is not much longer than a tweet.

Competition- Look at your competition before you start writing. Get an idea of their messages. You want to stand out and be better than they are.

Unique and relevant- Every page should have its own description that accurately describes that page. Make them compelling mini ads that accurately describe that page. This helps draw in targeted visitors.

Advertising Copy- The purpose of the META Description is to encourage people to click on the search engine result and come to your web page. Include a call to action to entice people to click through to your site. One technique is to include your phone number to encourage phone calls. Some people will call directly off the results page without clicking through to the site.

Keywords Unnecessary- Descriptions do not affect rankings. You do not need to worry about using keywords within your Description Tags. Titles should be crafted to entice people to click on your search result. Descriptions are more about conversion rather than SEO.

Length- Search engines will only display up to 160 characters. The optimal length of a description is 150-160 characters.

If we continue with our Orthodontist example, The Meta Description could be:

Dr. Arlene Novick specializes in Invisalign, Forsus & Traditional braces. Orthodontic office serving Los Angeles 90017 and surrounding areas. Call 213-XXX-XXXX

Using our Title and Description example, this would give a Google Search result that would look like:

Los Angeles Orthodontist, Invisalign | Dr. Arlene Novick

Dr. Arlene Novick specializes in Invisalign, Forsus & Traditional braces. Orthodontic office serving Los Angeles 90017 and surrounding areas. Call 213-XXX-XXXX

H1 Header Tag Best Practices

H1 Tags are the main web page headline. They should contain your most important keyword phrase and grab an arriving visitor's interest. Failing to use any H1 heading tags is a common SEO mistake. Many sites that have H1 headings, waste this important real estate with a very prominent WELCOME showing on their home page.

Headings are defined with the "<h1>" to "<h6>" tags. The H1 Header is the largest and the most important of these tags. Search engines put the most weight in H1 heading and it is regarded as the most important visible text on the web page.

Header Tag Optimization Tips

1. The main topic of the page should be the H1. Use H2 tags to break down the main topic into sub topics.

2. H1 tags should include the primary keyword phrase for the page. Additional keywords can be placed in the H2

tags. H3 tags carry only a minor importance with the search engines, so use sparingly with keywords.

3. Don't overuse the H1 and H2 tags. Each page should have only one H1 and one or two H2 tags. H4 thru H6 don't carry any real SEO weight.

4. Limit the length of each tag to a phrase or simple sentence. This is the same logic you would apply to any article headline.

5. Do not repeat keywords in these tags, as that will be flagged as spam. Avoid stuffing keywords in heading tags.

6. Words at the front of the heading tags are more important to the search engines.

How to Use Keywords

Use your keywords visibly on each web page for maximum benefit. Building these keywords into every facet of your website forms the messaging that allows you to better connect with your prospect.

1. Page URLs- Name pages with keywords phrases that describe the page. Separate keywords with hyphens.

2. Navigation- The navigation should be SEO friendly HTML links rather than JavaScript links or an image map. Use keywords as much as possible in the navigation links.

3. Breadcrumbs- These are a trail left so visitors will know their location. **Example: Home page > Product One > Installation Instructions.** Use breadcrumb navigation on larger sites that include keywords.

4. Title Tags- Each page should have unique Title tag. Keyword phrases should be at the beginning and the company name should be at the end.

5. Description and Keywords Tags- Use unique page descriptions and keywords tags for each page that accurately describes each web page.

6. H1/H2 Tags- H1 Tags are the main web page headline. They should contain your most important keyword phrase and grab an arriving visitor's interest. Additional keywords can be placed in the H2 tags.

7. Body Text- This is the page content. Each page of your website should have 250 or more words of text. Each page should include your most important keywords and if yours is a local business, your pages should show the cities that you serve.

8. Emphasized text- Within the content, use keywords in bold and italicized text, in bulleted lists and numbered lists. This makes them standout as important.

9. Internal Links- link to relevant internal pages using your keywords.

10. Images- Name images with your keyword phrase and use them in your ALT text.

Pay Per Click Advertising

Pay-per-click or PPC is a model used in Internet marketing. This is where you only pay when someone clicks on your ad. Examples are Google AdWords, Facebook ads, etc.

PPC can get great results fast or cause you to burn through a lot of money and get no results. The difference is in the planning and execution of your campaign. Here are some tips to maximize your PPC marketing efforts.

1. Keywords- Choose your keywords carefully. They should be highly relevant to your product or service. Don't just select popular phrases. **Longer phrases are better for getting PPC results.** Research shows that people just starting to learn about a subject will search using 1-2 word phrases. People ready to purchase or take action will search using specific 3-5 word phrases.

2. Ad Copy- Your ad is your initial entry to your landing page. It should include the specific keyword phrase the searcher used to find your ad. This means having a different ad for each keyword phrase (or group of keyword phrases) will increase your conversion rate.

3. Microsites or Website- In most other businesses, landing pages would be used. A landing page is a simplified web page with limited or no navigation links and is focused on getting your visitor to take a specific

action.

For dental and medical, PPC works better going to a website or microsite. Microsites would be a smaller version of the website, focused on a single special service. Microsites are a hybrid between a landing page and the full website.

It seems that patients don't trust landing pages and want to have a chance to look around the website before committing to a dentist for an appointment.

4. Call to action- Make it easy for your visitor to take action on your landing page. Locate your embedded form, action link or phone number where it is clearly visible and above the fold.

Use Social Media Optimization

Social Media Optimization or SMO is a form of word of mouth marketing through the use of social networking, social bookmarking, blogging and media sharing (photo, video) websites. The focus of SMO is on relationship and trust building. SMO is about increasing traffic flow to your social media content pages.

SMO focuses on securing traffic from sources other than search engines. When your content is placed on your website such as with a blog, traffic flow will increase to the website.

SMO is giving people a reason to visit and link to your site because of great original content. Links from social media back to your site are important for SEO. Improved search rankings are often a benefit of successful SMO.

Social media marketing is very different than traditional marketing. It's about publishing interesting content, creating relationships and trust. It's not about selling, though people do prefer to buy from those they know and trust.

Use social media to build your brand and your reputation, not to sell products. Brand yourself as a leader. Your brand is what you represent, what you care about and your connection to others. You want to be the unique and persuasive voice in your market. Your goal is to create a cultural following.

Social media participants can interact with you and learn your products or services in the process. Social media focuses on sharing content using RSS feeds, social news and sharing buttons, user rating and polling tools, and incorporating third-party community functionalities like images and videos. Sharing is made easy by adding social media sharing and bookmarking buttons along with your content.

Combine SMO with your SEO efforts. Use it to bring traffic to your website through links and gain better search engine rankings.

Your objective is to bring in more new patients. Your dental website will be the hub that all your marketing will send visitors to. Website traffic should come to your website multiple sources including digital and traditional marketing campaigns.

11 Metrics and KPIs

Once you make your website live, you will need to set up your measurement systems. These are the metrics and key performance indicators that will track your website performance.

In business if you want to improve say, employee performance, you set goals and measure performance. You may need to meet with them weekly, to guide them toward the results you want.

The same is true with your website. You need your website to deliver results. You need to set goals and measure performance. Only in the case of your website you will continue to make adjustments and watch how performance changes. In Chapter 12 we will discuss the ongoing work and changes you can make with your website.

Websites have the advantage that there are a tremendous number of things that can be measured. What is important is to boil these down to metrics that are meaningful and that will help you reach your business goals.

You will establish the major goals and the key measurements that show movement toward these goals. These are the KPIs, or Key Performance Indicators. Each KPI will have multiple metrics that will help you focus on how to improve it.

Key Performance Indicators

Remember all KPIs are metrics, but not all metrics are KPIs. KPIs are metrics that help steer toward your business goals. A KPI is a quantifiable measure of your marketing progress. You should focus on 3-4 of the most important metrics that will provide meaning at all levels of the organization.

Figure 11.1 Key Performance Indicators

To select the key performance indicators for your website you need to look back at the business purpose for your website. See Chapter 1.

What makes for a good key performance indicator?

1. It should inform how the business is doing
2. Be a measure of success or failure
3. Be decided upon by management
4. Be easily understood by all levels of the organization
5. Inspire action

By using these attributes of a good KPI, visits to your website or rankings in the search engines are not good KPIs. These are metrics that don't inform how the business is doing. They are not a measure of success or failure toward meeting goals.

Visits may be a supporting metric of the KPI transactions per day, or sales $ per day. Visits are only a small piece of the puzzle. To get a transaction you need a good volume of interested visitors. They need to be interested and engage well with the site and there needs to be a good conversion rate.

Visits are not close enough to the business goal to be considered a KPI.

Lead Generation

Let's say your number one business goal was to generate new dental patients for your practice through online appointment requests from web form submissions and phone calls.

Using Google Analytics you can track metrics such as the numbers of visits to any particular page. You can also track actions such as web form completions. Web form completions would be the number of visits to the thank you page after the web form has been completed.

Phone calls can be tracked by setting a unique phone number for the website that forwards to your main number. This is often called a call tracking phone number.

Then website key performance indicators could be-

1. New appointments from your website / week- This would be the total phone calls and form submissions.
2. Conversion rate- This is the total new appointments divided by website visits.
3. Web form abandonment rate- This is the percent of people that go to a form and then fail to complete it. A high abandonment rate means the web form is creating a barrier to conversions.

$$\text{Formula} = \frac{(\text{WEB FORM VISITS} - \text{THANK YOU PAGE VISITS})}{\text{WEB FORM VISITS}}$$

4. New customers acquired from the website. This could be online sales or converted leads.

5. PPC cost per lead- If you are using Google Adwords, track and reduce your $ spent divided by the number of leads.

6. Quantity and quality of online reviews. Track the number of new reviews on Google+, Yelp, Angie's list etc. You can use companies like reputology.com to monitor the review sites for you with both free and paid versions.

eCommerce Sales

Let's say your primary objective was direct sales from your website. This could be for products you are selling related to your practice. What would some possible KPIs be for this type of website?

1. Daily or weekly sales volume. This could be total sales $, units sold or sales $ by product line.

2. Conversion rate would be the visitors who purchase divided by the total number of website visitors.

3. Shopping cart abandonment rate. Track the number of people that start, but do not complete the purchase process divided by the number that starts the purchase process.

4. PPC conversion rate. This is the number of people that complete an action divided by the total number of people that click on an ad.

5. PPC cost per sale. These are the total dollars spent divided by the number of sales.

6. Affiliate performance rate. This could be the number of leads, sales $ or conversion rate.
7. Returns rate. Dollars or units returned for a time period divided by sales volume.
8. Quantity and quality of product reviews. Use this to remove the low performers and only keep the best rated products.

These KPIs will form the dashboard that allows you to quickly gauge your success or failure of your website and how visitors are engaging with it.

Use metrics to support KPIs

Use metrics that influence a KPI to help guide what changes and improvements you should make to your website. There may be dozens of underlying metrics that guide you toward an improvement on a KPI.

Suppose your KPI was to achieve a 2% conversion rate on your lead generation website. You would setup a series of metrics that could help improve the conversion rate.

If your conversion rate was 0.5%, what would you look for?

You could start by looking at how your website visitors are engaging with your website. Do they find your content interesting?

This is where using your website analytics such as Google Analytics comes in handy. You can analyze factors that lead to conversion such as bounce rate.

Bounce Rate is the percentage of visitors that leave without moving deeper into your website. These are the people who look only at a single page and then leave. A high bounce rate often leads to a lower conversion rate.

The exception to this is if you are sending traffic to a landing page as in a PPC campaign. Typical landing pages have no easy way to navigate to other pages so they have high bounce rates and still have good conversion rates.

Typical bounce rates for dental practice websites are 45%-55%. Ecommerce websites are typically lower at about 25%.

Ways to improve bounce rate include-

1. Verify you are targeting the right prospects with your keywords.
2. Add clear call to actions to move them into your selling sequence.
3. Make sure your call-to-actions are compelling and highly visible.
4. Rewrite and make your content more compelling.
5. Add videos to illustrate products or services in use.
6. Reorganize content to make it less confusing.
7. Format your information into shorter paragraphs.

8. Add trust elements such as trust logos, privacy policies, returns policies, product reviews, testimonials etc.

This is just one possible metric. Other visitor engagement metrics include-

- Average time on site. This is typically 2 min or longer.
- Average pages per visit. This should be as high as possible.
- Repeat visitors. Visitors that return are more engaged.

Google Analytics and Webmaster Tools

These are two free Google products that you should setup for your website to help gather your metrics data.

Google Analytics is the single most used analytics package for websites. This allows you to measure a huge number of metrics. It allows you to track conversions, sales funnel activity, detailed engagement by page, demographics information about your visitors and much much more.

Setup is easy. There is a tremendous amount of documentation and tutorials available to help you get the most out of it. You can even design a custom report and have them emailed to you automatically. Data can be exported to Excel making analysis easy.

Google Webmaster Tools gives you valuable measurements on the SEO health of your website. It shows what is working well and provides tools that will uncover the sources of a problem. This is a free Google tool and is even more powerful when you link it with your Google Analytics account.

1. Enable Email Notifications- Under preferences you can enable email notifications. You will generally receive no more than one email a day advising you of potential issues with your website.

2. HTML Improvements- Listed under the Search Appearance section. This will advise you of technical improvements that you can make to improve your search results. This includes Title Tags, Meta Descriptions and non-indexed content.

3. Search Queries- Listed under the Search Traffic section. Track how often your website is appearing in Googles search queries (impressions) and the click volume for each search phrase. It will Display your average search position for each phrase in the Google search results.

4. Links to Your Site- Also under the Search Traffic section. This will show the number of links coming to your site, from which websites and the link text (anchor text) that is being used.

5. Manual Actions- Hopefully this section is empty. This would be where a notification of penalty is posted if someone from the web spam team has determined that your website has violated Google's webmaster guidelines.

   If a manual action was imposed, details will be listed. You should address the problems. Your website should follow Google's webmaster guidelines. From within Webmaster Tools, you can then request a review by Google for reconsideration.

6. Index Status- Listed under the Google Index section. This shows the number of URL's that Google has been able to crawl and index. It will also show the numbers of URLs blocked by a robots.txt file.

   The robots.txt file is a simple text file that defines rules for search engines to crawl and index a site. It allows a site owner to specify which robots should crawl the site and which areas of their website should be left alone.

7. Crawl Errors. Listed under the crawl section. Track the pages not found (404 errors). This allows you to view which URLs are being "not found" and then to mark them as fixed.

8. Crawl Stats. Listed under the crawl section. There are a number of measurements, but I watch the average time spent downloading a page. This gives me a relative

measure of page load speed. If this trends upward, then you may be having a page load speed problem. For a more in depth look at page load speed go to Google's Page Speed Insights.

Studies have shown that web pages that take over 2 seconds to load will quickly lose visitors, particularly those on mobile devices. One study found that 18% of shopping cart abandonment was due to slow loading pages.

9. Sitemaps- Listed under the crawl section. Make sure Google has processed your XML sitemaps. You can submit new sitemaps here and view if there are any issues with your sitemaps.

While there are many more tools and metrics that you can look at, these are the main ones I track on a weekly basis.

Other free sources for metrics

SEOQuake tool bar- This is a free add-on for your browser. This can be installed on most major browsers such a Chrome, Firefox, Opera and Safari. The Toolbar provides metrics such Alexa Rank, pages indexed by Google, Title tags, META descriptions, keyword density, text volume, etc. for a web page you navigate to.

Keep this plugin off until you arrive to a page you want to analyze. Then turn it on and refresh the

*page. If you leave it on, it will make too many queries
and Google is likely to ban your computer from doing
searches for a short time.*

MajesticSEO.com- This website has some powerful link
popularity analysis tools. There are free and paid options.
The free version provides many excellent reports and
analysis on most websites.

OpenSiteExplorer.org. This is another website that provides
link popularity or backlink analysis on most any website.
There are free and paid versions and these metrics are
different than MajesticSEO.com.

SEMrush.com- Provides all sorts of traffic and keywords
metrics. There are free and paid plans. Great source for
doing an analysis of your competitors sites as well as
gathering metrics on your own website.

Woorank.com- This site does an online website analysis. It
will pull together over 50 different metrics and prepare a
report for you. You can run one free analysis per week or
purchase one of their paid plans if you are tracking multiple
websites.

Baseline metrics

Once your website goes live, record baseline values for each of your metrics and KPIs. This gives you the starting point. Schedule a weekly time to record the new values for each.

An easy way to track this is to setup an Excel spreadsheet and keep adding columns for each new weekly measurement. From here you can add graphs that allow you to visually see trends.

———————

Websites have the advantage that there are a tremendous number of things that can be measured. What is important is to boil these down to metrics that are meaningful and that will help you reach your business goals.

12   After Your Site Goes Live

Once your website goes live, your work has only begun. Your website is an important marketing tool that serves as a connection to your prospects and patients.

Websites must be updated; new content added regularly, changes made to improve performance of KPIs and metrics. The worst thing you can do is to get your website project completed and then set it aside and forget about it.

Your first thought may be that you don't have time for this. But isn't getting new patients into your practice critical for your success?

You can outsource some of the routine work, but someone on your team must take responsibility for the oversight of your website performance.

You need to assign the ongoing maintenance and improvement of your site to a key person in your organization. This is usually someone with marketing responsibilities.

What should your ongoing website marketing include? You need to develop your own process based on your dental practice goals and the competitiveness of your market.

Remember the technology and competition in website marketing is always advancing just like it is in dentistry. It takes a lot of time and effort for you to reach and maintain a leadership position on the web.

Setup a regular website review meeting to track results and agree on action plans. For most larger dental clinics, this is a formal monthly meeting.

Figure 12.1 Monthly Website Review

There are seven areas that you should design your ongoing website marketing program around. Each month review your accomplishments and spend time redefining your next month's action plan.

1. Monitor and measure
2. Keep content updated
3. Improve conversions
4. Grow your traffic base
5. Grow your content
6. Add reviews and testimonials
7. Monitor your competition

Monitor and measure

Use your KPIs and metrics you defined in Chapter 11 and begin systematically recording your metrics and monitor your progression toward your goals.

You will quickly see that some of your metrics provide valuable insights that help you make improvements. Other metrics are just meaningless information.

At least monthly, evaluate if your measurements are meaningful. If they are not, prune away the ones that are not helping improve and add new ones that will.

You are creating a standard system for continual improvement of your website. This is often called the PDCA cycle used in process improvement.

Plan- Identify opportunities to create action plans for change.

Do- Make small scale changes based on your plans.

Check- Use metrics data to see if the change made a difference.

Act- If successful, keep the change and use on a wider scale. If unsuccessful, begin the cycle again.

Your website marketing will be fluid and ever changing. Use performance measurements to guide your website to get better and better results.

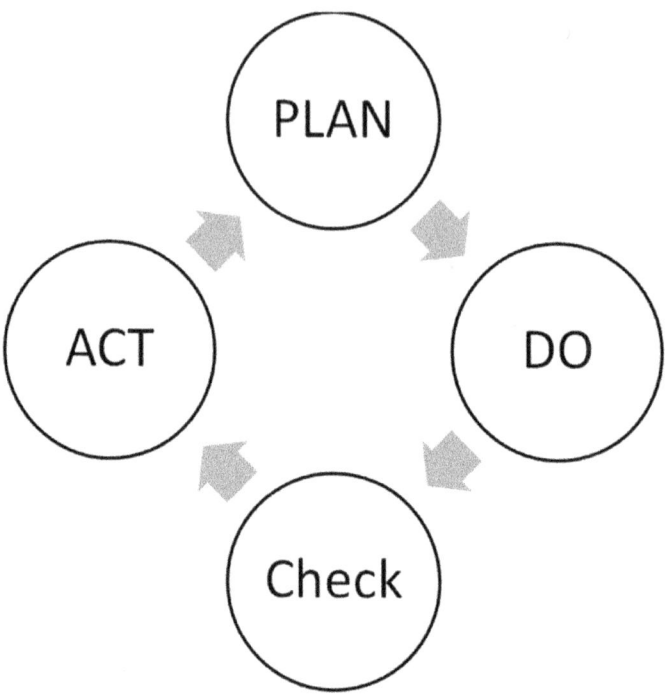

Figure 12.2 PDCA Cycle

Keep content updated

Your website should demonstrate the value your business offers to prospective patients. A stale outdated website sends the wrong message about your dental practice.

Savvy web visitors can quickly spot old content. This is the difference between a brochure and a newspaper. Current and timely is better.

Fresh, new content helps keep visitors engaged and coming back. For ideas, monitor what your competition is doing to keep their sites fresh. Borrow the best ideas and apply to your website.

There is nothing worse than prominently posting your April special on your site when it is currently July.

Your website will have two types of content. Content that change slowly such as the About Us or FAQ pages. Then there are web pages that are likely to change regularly such as specials, products and services, meet the team and in the news pages.

Guidelines for evaluating content

- Update or remove outdated information.

- Fix spelling and grammatical errors. You can run a spell checker over your entire website.

- Avoid large blocks of text. Paragraphs should be brief with 1-4 sentences per paragraph.

If your website has a blog, make sure new postings are written regularly. Certainly no less that once per month.

If your website offers specials, update and change at least monthly to encourage return visits.

Make it part of your monthly website review to identify outdated content and to replace them or update them. Constantly adding new and fresh content will help your search engine rankings.

As part of your regular website maintenance check monthly for broken links by running a scan of the site. Check for 404 errors which indicate the need to add 301 redirects. Google Webmaster Tools is a good place to check this.

At least quarterly check how your website looks with the latest browsers. Sometimes new browsers will "break" some graphic on your website. Usually this is a simple fix, but you want to keep your website looking good to your website visitors. Use a tool like browsershots.org to check a few key pages.

Improve conversions

You want to make it easy for your visitors reach to reach their objectives. This could be to buy from you or at least engage with your business. Your initial call to actions and selling sequence is only a best guess and a good starting point.

You will want to use metrics to guide you in making changes. One of your first steps is to identify and optimize your conversion funnel.

These are the steps from arriving to your website, learning about what you offer, taking action and then arriving onto your thank You page.

In Google Analytics you can identify your conversion funnel by entering the page URL of each step. You will be able to see the fall off of people as they progress through your conversion steps.

Your job is to entice and guide your visitor through your conversion process. Design and optimize your path for your best patient. Use the information from your funnel metrics to optimize the conversion of each step.

Conversion tips

1. Make call-to-action clear and compelling

2. Show the benefits and provide proof in the form of reviews and testimonials.

3. Remove any friction points. These are points where they have to change from page to page, forms that require too much information. Your goal is to simplify.

Conversion improvement is best done by making many small changes and watching the impact of each change before moving onto the next one.

Another technique to improve conversions is called remarketing. This involves regular emailing of special offers to people who have registered on your website to receive these offers.

Typically companies will offer free shipping on the first order to a new customer if they elect to sign up to receive these email notifications of deals and offers.

You would then email your list weekly on special deals. People that arrive to your website from these emails are ready to buy. Your conversion rate and total sales increase with this technique.

Grow your traffic base

Traffic to your website will come from multiple sources. Each will behave differently. You will probably receive organic search traffic, referrals from other websites, visitors from your social media and paid advertising from each of your campaigns.

You need to look at each source in detail to understand what you may want to change.

Identify each source of traffic to your website using Google Analytics (or other analytics). Look at each source for not only how many visits there are, but also how the traffic engages with your website (bounce rate, visit duration, and number of pages per visit)

If you are looking at traffic from organic search traffic, look at which phrase are bringing the best traffic that engages well on your site. Which pages are they entering your site on? Which pages are they exiting on? Spend time with your analytics package and it will begin to tell a story of which traffic is engaging well with your site.

Make small changes and sit back and watch for improvement. Keep the changes that work.

You can keep adding new traffic channels, perhaps an affiliate program, perhaps banner advertising with some association you are a member of.

With analytics you can track the quantity and quality of the traffic and decide if it is worth investing more time or advertising dollars.

Grow your content

Content growth strategies such as adding a blog to your website is very important in today's SEO. Use blogs, press releases, articles and new product sections as ways to regularly grow your website content.

Adding a blog to your website is a powerful way to improve your website SEO and grow content. This involves a technique known as SEO Blogging. Each posting adds one more page of fresh original, keyword rich content to your website.

In SEO Blogging you use blogging to optimize your website. It requires writing interesting and original material to attract links from other bloggers. Here is how the process works.

1. Set-up a blog on your website. Place it in a folder such as mydomain.com/blog (never in a subdomain such as blog.mydomain.com). This is very important since others will link to your content and you want those links to benefit your entire website and not just your blog.

2. Keyword plan- Create a list of keywords that you want your website to rank well for. Every phrase should have a page on your website that it relates to. Place the URL of the page next to the keyword phrase that most closely relates to that phrase. For the best results you should be using these keyword phrases visibly on the content in your web pages.

3. Topic- Select a topic that interests you and that you think your readers will enjoy. The topic should be closely related to a keyword phrase from your keyword plan; this should be in line with the theme of your blog. Your blog should answer a popular question, solve a problem or entertain your audience.

4. Keyword Focused Posting- The key is to have a highly keyword focused posting that will link to a specific page on your site. Select one primary keyword phrase that you will center your entire posting around. Use the keyword in the title, in the first paragraph, at least one other time in the posting and once as a hyperlink to the most relevant page on your website.

For SEO Blogging, make it easy for readers to be able to scan through your content quickly and easily. A typical blog posting should be about 250 words and be written in a simple format.

To build an audience you should post 1-2 times per week and stay focused around your primary blog topic.

Add reviews and testimonials

Customer reviews need to be an important part of your marketing effort. These are reviews that your customers will leave on Google+, Yelp, Angie's List, etc.

These reviews provide the social proof that you are a reputable dentist to work with. Many of these sites will provide ratings that your prospective patients will use as part of their decision on who to go to.

Adding reviews should be part of your marketing effort. Some practices automatically send postcards or emails along with every appointment asking for their patients to leave a review.

To manage these reviews you should monitor any new reviews that are placed on these review sites and immediately respond to any negative review and try and turn around an unhappy patient. These review sites will allow the person that submits a review to change it.

Reputation management companies help make checking review sites easy. Reputology for example can be setup to email you daily with updates from the 5 major review sites.

Provide written and video patient testimonials on your website. An easy way to get these testimonials is to request feedback on every interaction.

You will want to obtain written consent to publish these testimonials. The easy way is to create a patient testimonial form with the consent and a signature line at the bottom of the form.

One very good system that I have seen sends a feedback request for every transaction. Positive feedback sends the person to a page encouraging them to leave a review on Yelp or Google+. Negative reviews are sent to a thank you page telling them that their concerns will be responded to.

Monitor your competition

Setup a system where you review your competition's websites, social media and paid advertising so you can track what they are doing.

Look at any new offerings. Set up some metrics to see if they are launching any new Internet marketing initiatives.

A few simple metrics recorded down every few months will alert you to which competitors are getting more aggressive in their marketing.

Here is a simple competitor analysis that can be done in less than 5 minutes per competitor website.

1. SEOQuake toolbar

    a. Alexa traffic ranking will indicate more website traffic going to their website.

    b. Pages indexed by Google- if this is growing, have they implemented a content growth strategy

2. SEMrush.com

    a. Search Engine Traffic shows the estimated traffic from organic search (first 2 pages of results)

    b. This source will show you if they are using PPC and what ads they are using

A simple analysis that only shows 2-3 metrics is all you need to see which competitors expanding their marketing effort.

————————

Once your website goes live, your work has only begun. Websites must be updated; new content added regularly, changes made to improve performance of KPIs and metrics.

You can outsource some of the routine work, but someone on your team must take responsibility for the oversight of your website performance.

Website Planning Checklist

Refer to the chapter shown for more information.

- ☐ Describe why you want this new website (Ch 1)
- ☐ What are your business marketing objectives (Ch 1)
- ☐ Describe purpose and objectives for website (Ch 1)

- ☐ Describe your best patient. (Ch 2)
- ☐ Develop patient profiles or personas. (Ch 2)
- ☐ Do keyword research and rate for rele
- ☐ Dentalvance. (Ch 2)
- ☐ Settle on your domain name. (Ch 3)

- ☐ Decide if you will keep or update your logo. Then get a high resolution version for your website design. (Ch 3)

- ☐ Decide what colors to use in branding. (Ch 3)

- ☐ Map out selling sequences by patient type. (Ch 4)
- ☐ Create a prioritized list of actions for visitors. (Ch 4)
- ☐ List out ways you will reassure visitors and build trust. (Ch 4)
- ☐ Create an inventory of videos you will use. (Ch 4)
- ☐ Integrate educational marketing? (Ch 4)

- ☐ List 3-5 reference websites. Include comments of what you like and what you don't like. (Ch 5)
- ☐ List of functions and features to include. (Ch 5)

- ☐ Do a competitive traffic review and compare your website to your competition. (Ch 5)

- ☐ Create the sitemap for your website. (Ch 6)

- ☐ Create the SEO Plan for your website. (Ch 6, 10)

- ☐ Create the wireframe for your home page. (Ch 6)

- ☐ Prepare the design brief completing as much information as possible. (Ch 6)

- ☐ Write the content for your Home Page. (Ch 7)
- ☐ Write the content for your About Us page. (Ch 7)
- ☐ Set a schedule to write the remainder of your website. (Ch 7)
- ☐ Decide if you will have separate mobile websites or use a responsive web design. (Ch 8)
- ☐ Which features are your priorities for your mobile visitor? (Ch 8)
- ☐ Decide if mobile phone users will see all text content or only high priority content. (Ch 8)

- ☐ Hire a Web Designer / Developer. (Ch 9)
- ☐ Buy off on design concepts. (Ch 9)
- ☐ Do final testing before site going live. (Ch 9)
- ☐ Identify a minimum of 3 traffic sources for your website. (Ch 10)
- ☐ Complete your SEO Plan. (Ch 10)

- ☐ Apply SEO to each web page using Your SEO plan as your guide. (Ch 10)
- ☐ Identify 3-4 KPIs that will support your business goals. (Ch 11)
- ☐ For each KPI, identify 3-5 metrics that will influence KPI performance. (Ch 11)
- ☐ Setup Google Analytics and Google Webmaster tools for your website. (Ch 11)
- ☐ Gather baseline metrics as your website goes live. (Ch 11)
- ☐ Assign responsibility for someone to be in charge of managing and improving the website results. (Ch 12)
- ☐ Setup monthly review meetings with your marketing team to review KPIs, metrics, results and action plans. (Ch 12)
- ☐ Implement a strategy to regularly add new content to your website. (Ch 12)
- ☐ Setup a quarterly review of your competitor websites to spot changes in their online marketing. (Ch 12)

References and Sources

1. *How we got from 1 to 162 million websites on the internet*, http://royal.pingdom.com/2008/04/04/how-we-got-from-1-to-162-million-websites-on-the-internet/ ,data accessed December 2015.

2. November 2015 Web Server Survey, http://news.netcraft.com/archives/2015/11/16/november-2015-web-server-survey.html , data accessed December 2015.

3. Pew Research Center Internet User Demographics, http://www.pewinternet.org/data-trend/internet-use/latest-stats/ , data accessed December 2015.

4. Keyword research using Market Samurai. Search keyword = dentist , data accessed December 2015.

5. Nick's Story, http://nickfriedman.com/about/, Data accessed December 2015.

6. Stanford Web Credibility Research, http://credibility.stanford.edu/guidelines/index.html, Data accessed Jan 2011.

7. Market Share of TLD Extensions, http://www.domainstate.com/registrar-tld-breakup.html, Data accessed December 2015.

8. Web users judge sites in the blink of an eye, http://www.nature.com/news/2006/060109/full/new s060109-13.html , data accessed April 2014.

9. A Study on How Much Mobile Traffic is going to Small Business Websites, http://www.dougwilliams.com/study-much-mobile-traffic-going-small-business-websites/, written by Doug Williams May 2014.

10. Post PC era in the US, http://ondeviceresearch.com/blog/post-pc-era-in-the-us-#sthash.HKJxpFZY.OnzXB1tP.dpbs, data accessed May 2014.

11. Infographic- Mobile Search Statistics, http://icebreakerconsulting.com/infographic-mobile-search-statistics/ data accessed May 2014.

12. 30+ compelling mobile search statistics, https://econsultancy.com/blog/63230-30-compelling-mobile-search-statistics#i.s55dk5630eirpj data accessed May 2014.

13. Building Smartphone-Optimized Websites, https://developers.google.com/webmasters/smartphone-sites/details data accessed May 2014.

14. Desktop Search Engine Market Share, https://www.netmarketshare.com/search-engine-

market-share.aspx?qprid=4&qpcustomd=0, data accessed January 2016.

Index

About the Author

Doug Williams

Doug Williams is president of Doug Williams Digital Marketing. He has started, grown and sold businesses, including a web development business. He has over 35 years of senior management experience, served on boards of directors and been a successful business consultant.

Doug Williams has been providing SEO and website planning services since 2002. What began as SEO for his own business consulting practice quickly grew into a SEO business. Then it grew into a 15 person Internet marketing business providing SEO services, website design and Internet marketing consulting.

In 2002, Doug Williams founded Doug Williams and Associates (DWA); a Website marketing company / Website building business with its core mission to help businesses grow. Doug has worked with many industry leaders to provide Internet marketing services to their clients. One of his special niches were medical and dental websites.

In 2010 Doug sold his website marketing business to a larger website company that focused on producing high quality websites to major businesses.

In 2013 Doug started Doug Williams Digital Marketing which is a boutique digital marketing agency that provides premium quality digital marketing strategy consulting and premium websites to a small group of clients.

Prior to becoming a consultant, Doug spent much of his career in management, 22 of these years in senior management positions across a wide range of industries. During this time, Doug defined and put in place many key business systems and improvement strategies to create profitable operations.

Doug has an MBA from Pepperdine University. His Undergraduate degree was in Biology and Chemistry as he pursued premed studies and applied to medical school.

Books Written by Doug Williams

    Biz Blog Marketing 2008
    Website Marketing Mastery 2010
    Mastering Blog marketing 2011
    SEO Made Easy 2012 eBook
    Dominate! 2014
    The Ultimate Dental Website 2016

Need Help With Your Marketing?

Hi, this is Doug Williams and I want to thank you for taking the next step in growing your dental practice. I have put some of my best stuff into this book in the hopes that you can put it to good use and prosper.

If you would like to take another step forward, go to my website DougWilliams.com and contact me to set up a time to talk to see if we can help you with your plans.

I look forward to meeting you!

Doug